CHARLIE WHITE'S
101 FISHING SECRETS

By Charles White
Illustrations by Nelson Dewey

CHARLIE WHITE'S
101 FISHING SECRETS

By Charles White
Illustrations by Nelson Dewey

A Maclean Hunter
Publication

Special Interest Publications

Special Interest Publications
A Division of Maclean Hunter Ltd.
#202 - 1132 Hamilton Street,
Vancouver, British Columbia

Canadian Cataloguing in Publication Data

White, Charles, 1925-
  Charlie White's 101 fishing secrets

(BC outdoors Saltaire series)
ISBN 0-88896-153-7

1. Fishing. 2. Fishing - British Columbia.
I. Title. II. Title: 101 fishing secrets. III. Series.
SH441.W48 1985   799.1   C85-091157-5

Cover Design: Wardle & Associates
Inside Book Design: Beach House Graphics
Printed and Bound in Canada: The Jasper Printing Group

I dedicate this book to my mother who has supported and encouraged me in my interest in fishing and wildlife since my "fishing fever" began when I was five years old. She tolerated my 3 a.m. departures for the local pond, the messy basement washtubs where I cleaned the catch, and even the hooks and worms left in my pockets.

She has survived it all, and I'm planning a gala salmon dinner for her on her eighty-third birthday in June.

Acknowledgements

Everyone who taught me something about fishing, and that includes *all* my fishing partners, deserves my thanks because I learn something on every fishing trip. Special thanks to Rhys Davis, Charlie Guiguet, and Lee and Patty Hallberg, who showed me the basics of salmon fishing.

Thanks also to those who helped develop the underwater TV system which revealed so much about salmon behavior: Allan Hook, Roger and Tony Rose, Nick Dominique, Laraine Frances, Mike Shack, Bruce Colegrave, Jack Lugg, my sons Chad, Kevin and David, and the gang at Sony.

I also want to acknowledge those who did so much in preparation of this book — Nelson Dewey, Sally Constable, Tim Cyr, Rex Armstead, Mary S. Aikins and the staff at Special Interest Publications.

— Charlie White

Contents

Introduction 11

CHAPTER 1
General Considerations 19

CHAPTER 2
Preparing for a Fishing Trip 29

CHAPTER 3
Finding the Fish 43

CHAPTER 4
Between You and the Bottom 57

CHAPTER 5
Trolling Techniques 75

CHAPTER 6
Fishing with Bait 97

CHAPTER 7
Mature Salmon in River Mouth Areas 103

CHAPTER 8
Striking, Playing and Landing a Fish 111

CHAPTER 9
Future Plans 128

INTRODUCTION

Webster's Dictionary has many definitions of the word "secret", the most prominent of which is "kept from knowledge or view", "something kept hidden or unexplained". Another — "revealed only to the initiated" — is more appropriate in this instance since much of the information in this book is already known to experienced and so-called "expert" anglers.

This book is a compilation of the tips and "secrets" I learned

from experts when I first started fishing; the knowledge I have acquired from my own fishing experiences and especially the things I have learned and continue to learn from my research with an underwater television camera.

Boyhood experiences

I have been fishing for more than 50 years, having started with a bobber and worm in the ponds and streams of Pennsylvania and Ohio when I was six years old. For the next 20 years I fished enthusiastically for carp, catfish, sunfish, blue gills, creek suckers, chubs, rock bass, walleye, pike and perch. I even had the occasional battle with smallmouth and largemouth bass.

On several occasions I traveled to Ontario for some exciting fishing for larger bass, great northern pike, and deep-running lake trout. During a stint with the U.S. Navy, I fished for cod off Nova Scotia.

Life cycle studies

In those days, fishing was the most intense of a number of personal hobbies, but became the core of my life only after I moved to the west coast in 1948. I became obsessed with salmon fishing, ultimately spending two years with the Oregon Fish Commission as a biologist-photographer. I fin-clipped young salmon in hatcheries and then followed them through their entire life cycle. I learned a great deal from the other biologists who were also keen anglers in their spare time.

After moving to Vancouver Island, British Columbia, in 1956, fishing became even more important to me. I had moved to

Victoria primarily to build and operate a television station, but there is no doubt that my move was strongly influenced by the good fishing nearby.

Fishing guide

When the station was completed, I moved full-time into fishing projects. I operated a fishing charter business during the summer and designed marine products (crab traps, sinkers and bait boxes) during the off-season.

Being a guide was not the easy-going occupation I thought it would be. In fact, being a guide can entail more pressure than that experienced by most business executives. Yet I quickly established a reputation for consistent success using light tackle (much sport fishing in those days was done with heavy wire lines and cannon balls) and attracted many "executive parties" from such places as Victoria's Empress Hotel and through the tourist bureau.

Some groups would fly in by private jet, rush by taxi to the

marina, and we would be off to the fishing grounds. If we didn't
have a fish in the boat within the first 30 minutes, some of the
high-powered execs would begin tapping their feet on the deck
and strumming their fingers on the arms of their seats. Not a
word was spoken (usually), but I knew they were thinking
"Well, Mr. Expert, where's the fish?" Mercifully, the fishing
was usually pretty good and I had developed some quite successful strategies which I will explain later in the book. There
were, however, too many occasions when the fishing was really
"tough", and my tension level soared as I scrambled to get that
first fish on board.

There are no relaxing days on the water. The customer
doesn't really care about the big catch you made last week, or
the exciting run of giant salmon due at the end of the month. He
wants fish in the box today!

All this activity was a far cry from my formal education: I had
obtained a degree in Civil Engineering from Cornell University
in New York state, and then practised engineering for two years
prior to my move to the west coast. This training gave me the
necessary background to develop an exciting new project. This
project was conceived while talking with charter guests who
regularly expressed great curiosity, not only about salmon, but
about all marine life and the underwater environment.

Undersea observations

The project was the development of the Undersea Gardens, a unique marine exhibit something like an aquarium in reverse. Essentially it is a large steel chamber in which the public descends and watches marine life in a more natural environment. A fence around the chamber holds marine creatures close enough for viewing.

After building the first Undersea Gardens (four were eventually constructed, one each in British Columbia, Washington, Oregon and California), I spent hundreds of hours watching salmon and other marine creatures. I learned about their feeding habits in relation to tidal action, time of day and availability of

food. I was not, however, completely satisfied with these observations, and continued to look for a way to observe salmon behavior, underwater, in the wild.

Then one day while shopping at a local drug store, I noticed a small surveillance camera used to detect shoplifters. Suddenly I was struck with the idea of using such a camera underwater. I was developing the Scotty Downrigger at the time and thought that I could hook this tiny camera on the downrigger wire and watch my lures in action. We designed and constructed a special housing and lowered the apparatus under my boat. The first unit leaked and a mass of foam boiled out of the housing when we opened it. Salt water, electric current and delicate circuit boards just don't mix.

The next housing worked well enough, but we got nothing but pictures of the bottom of the boat and propellers. Finally we got it working, then spent months overcoming control problems so we could keep the camera aimed at the trolling lure.

I'll never forget the first time everything worked properly. I was sitting in the cockpit of the boat watching a television monitor as my lure moved through the water almost 40 feet below. My dream was actually coming true. I could watch what every fisherman has dreamed of ... the actual moment of strike.

As we watched the screen a fish suddenly loomed behind the lure. At first we couldn't figure out what kind of fish it was, but then realized it was a salmon. But the salmon was swimming *upside down*, approaching the lure on its back. We were so excited that the helmsman left the wheel and the boat began weaving in slow circles around the bay.

The fish approached the lure several times, then veered off. We thought we had already made a dramatic discovery about salmon behavior. They apparently rolled over onto their backs to strike a lure. This seemed possible when I remembered films about sharks in the South Pacific, footage that showed them rolling over on their backs to attack the belly of a fleeing bait fish.

We quickly hauled the gear to the surface so we could rush off and announce our exciting new discovery to the whole fishing

world. But when we got the gear to the surface, we discovered that the cables had tangled, and it was the *camera* that was upside down.

After a lot more trial and error, we got the system operating reasonably well and began to learn some things that fishermen have wondered about for thousands of years. For the first time, we were able to watch, in close up and slow-motion, as fish approached and struck (or turned away from) our lures.

Almost immediately we debunked one of the most prevalent theories of most fishing experts. Popular wisdom had it that a salmon always grabbed a bait or lure by the head (to kill it, they said), since they often found teeth marks near the front end of lures. However, our camera showed that salmon consistently grabbed all lures from the tail. Even those which approached the lure from the side would usually circle around from behind and attack directly from the rear. This had all kinds of implications for lure design and hook placement.

We also disproved the theory that salmon slapped the bait with their tail before striking. We often saw salmon rush a lure then turn away at the last minute with their tails whipping past the lure. However, on closer scrutiny of these shots in slow motion, we found that the fish never touched the lure. Apparently they were just giving it a close inspection and turning away at the last possible moment.

In analyzing these same shots we discovered that the fish always passed with its lateral line in close proximity to the moving lure. Biologists speculate that they are somehow sensing the vibration or density of the lure with their lateral line as they pass close to it. We hope to investigate this phenomenon more thoroughly to help us in future lure design.

We also made some discoveries about the importance of sharp hooks, proper fishing depth, and lure action, but we will cover these in the main body of the book.

Chapter 1
General Considerations

Several years ago a most unusual book became a best seller. It was titled *Inner Tennis* and dealt with the importance of attitude and confidence in improving your game. There is no doubt that a positive attitude is also extremely important to fishing success. If you expect success, you are much more likely to have it. This is true in tennis, fishing or almost any human activity. This, then, is my first secret to successful fishing.

| 1 | **A POSITIVE ATTITUDE** |

The person who expects success when he goes fishing will approach the sport with enthusiasm and take the time to do

things right. Since he expects a strike, he is going to be sure that his lure is right, his knots are properly tied and that his landing net is ready for the big one.

It is interesting to watch the weekend "duffer" as he heads

out onto the water only half prepared. Basically this is because he feels defeated before he even starts out.

How do you get that positive feeling, that expectation of success? It comes partly from successful experience and partly from learning from others, watching films on fish behavior and from reading books like this one. Indeed, one of the objectives of this book is to provide some of that feeling of confidence.

2 | ATTENTION TO DETAIL

This could also be called fastidiousness, fussiness, perfectionism or any other of a number of labels for the person who checks and double-checks every detail.

Successful fishing is not a "laid back" sport. It requires that you do perhaps 20 or 25 little things all exactly right. Any weak link in the chain or a forgotten item will often result in getting skunked.

Any fisherman can stumble onto a fish by just trolling around with his feet up while he sips on a beer. And while this may give him a pleasant day in the sun, it won't bring consistent fishing success.

This may sound discouraging for those who look on fishing as a pleasant and relaxed outing. However, once you get in the habit of taking care of all of the little details, they become almost automatic and fishing becomes even more pleasant, because now you are catching fish, which is the object of the exercise in the first place.

| **3** | **PERSISTENCE IS IMPORTANT** |

Successful fishing requires persistent effort. There is no substitute for spending time on the water, working your lures

and working the likely fishing spots. The man who catches the most fish often spends the most hours with his line in the water.

Even the so-called experts get skunked more often than any of them will admit. Remember, if the fish aren't there, no one will catch them.

Even when there are fish in the area, often they just will not bite. My underwater camera shows that more than 90 per cent of the fish which approach a lure will turn away without striking. Biologists feel this is because the fish are not hungry. (And how many more don't even approach the lure because they feel satiated?)

One biologist told me that he believed a salmon will feed

actively once a day for approximately 45 minutes, with another shorter feeding time of half an hour or less. The rest of the time is spent in digesting the food.

We can often predict these feeding times with some accuracy, but other times we cannot. As Charlie Giuguet, a top biologist and expert fisherman once told me, "Charlie, you just have to keep going out on the water."

4 KEEP RECORDS

Salmon and most marine creatures have a regular and predictable life cycle. Feeding habits, migrations, preferred habitat and even depth and color preferences vary with the time of year in a somewhat predictable manner.

For the past 25 years, I have kept records of almost every salmon I have caught, listing all pertinent information in a diary or log book. The records are kept in a manner which allows direct comparison with the same date or week each year.

For example, all of my catches for the third week in August over the past 25 years are listed together. This allows me an

instant year-by-year comparison of my catches during that week. After several years, a pattern emerged which is extremely helpful in planning my fishing during that time of year. For instance, perhaps I will note that fish are likely to be at 100 to 130 feet deep, they prefer small spoons and the "bite" usually takes place during the small, evening ebb tides. Because the bait fish have similar annual patterns, we also learn that a certain size lure is most effective because it matches the natural growth cycle of the feed at that time of year.

Of course, the most important information such a diary provides is *where* the fish will be found. These seasonal migration

patterns are extremely regular and the salmon seem to show up almost like clockwork at the same spots during a certain week each year.

During spawning migrations this is in response to the salmon's biological clock; the eggs and spawn ripen within the fish's body and push him toward his birthplace. Even during their active feeding growth cycle, the salmon follow the bait fish (herring, anchovies, needlefish) which also move in response to a seasonal pattern as they follow the plankton, water temperatures and other factors. This means that concentrations of bait will show up at the same times and places each year and will surely be followed by the salmon.

You can use a spiral bound notebook as a diary, or use one of the commercially available fishing log books. My own version is shown at the end of this volume.

5 | BECOME A SPECIALIST

Fishing can become frustrating for anyone when the fish don't co-operate or when they just aren't there at all. This leads many fishermen to try virtually every lure in the tackle

store in an attempt to catch fish by "throwing everything at them".

It often does make good sense to change your approach (see Secret 6), but it is almost impossible for anyone, especially a part-time fisherman, to master all of the intricacies of all the various lures and fishing methods available today.

We all must specialize to some extent. Because my underwater camera works best when trolling, I have become a specialist in trolling and have even narrowed my lure choices. I use a lot of natural baits (herring, herring strip, anchovies) and I love to use bucktail flies with mother-of-pearl spinners when the coho are around. I also use long, narrow spoons on sandy bottoms for needlefish and wider spoons when fishing in areas of small herring. I also troll with my downrigger most of the time.

A number of my fishing friends have moved almost exclusively to drift fishing while others will specialize in using certain flashers or dodgers in combination with hoochies, bait or spoons. Only by specializing in certain techniques can you master the fine points which will improve your productivity.

Becoming a specialist also means specializing in certain fish-

ing locations. It is far better to learn a few locations well than to rush around to a different spot every weekend and not learn those special "holding spots" for fish. I think that intimate knowledge of specific fishing areas is one of the most important secrets an angler can have. I know of a number of special drop-offs, places where tidal currents interact, and even flat sandbars where fish seem to congregate. I have learned these special spots only from repeated trips to the same areas.

6 | FLEXIBILITY A KEY

While this may seem to contradict the secrets outlined above, it is important to keep yourself flexible enough to change tactics when necessary. Don't follow too rigid an approach.

For instance, if you are trolling with herring strip and see fish being taken by other boats on flasher and hoochie it makes sense to switch to another combination which might be more productive. Before changing lures, though, it is a good idea to make sure

that you are fishing at the same depth as the other anglers. Often, getting to the right depth will allow you to catch fish on many different lure combinations.

The same holds true for location. You might be convinced that fishing a certain drop-off is most productive, but then you might see fish "signs" (diving birds, seagulls, bait fish or salmon jumping) which should lead you to investigate another spot.

I remember a dramatic incident at a fishing camp in Rivers Inlet, the fabled trophy salmon area along B.C.'s northern coast. Shortly after noon, a new group of fishermen had flown in from Vancouver eager to try their luck. Those of us who had been there several days had been fishing hard all morning and were preparing for an afternoon snooze.

The new arrivals were keen to get on the water and loaded their small putter boats with gear and bait for a mid-afternoon expedition. The "experienced" group watched with a chuckle as the newcomers took off. "They'll learn," we mused, "those fish aren't likely to bite in the lazy midday hours."

Two hours later we awoke from our naps to excited cries from

the returning boats. Our eyes popped out as we watched three huge salmon being lifted from the boats and dragged to the weigh-in scales. Two of the salmon tipped the scales at over 70 pounds. They turned out to be the largest salmon taken in all of B.C. that year.

And they were taken between one and three in the afternoon,

which all the conventional wisdom would say was a dead fishing time. For the next 10 days there were no afternoon naps as the waters of Rivers Inlet were whipped to a froth all day long by every angler in camp! You just never know. You have to stay flexible.

On another occasion I was showing one of my underwater salmon behavior films to an audience in Campbell River, B.C., where many professional guides make a good living helping tourists catch fish. One of the guides approached me after the show with a puzzled expression on his face. "Charlie," he said, "you showed those salmon grabbing the herring by the tail."

"Yes?" I replied.

"Well, they just don't do that," he muttered.

"Do you think I faked the pictures?" I said, smiling.

"I don't know what you did, but they just don't do that."

Here was a man, a professional, whose ideas were so fixed that he could not believe or accept a new idea, even with photographic evidence.

Chapter 2
Preparing for a Fishing Trip

Many anglers give no consideration at all to preparations for a fishing trip. They just get up in the morning, grab their clothes, rod and tackle box and take off for the boat. However, proper planning and preparation can have a substantial impact on fishing success.

7 | USE QUALITY EQUIPMENT

Most of us who started fishing as children used hand-me-down equipment or maybe an inexpensive rod and reel bought through a promotional special. I'm sure we had a wonderful time fishing with this tackle, but on the other hand cheaply made gear can break down at critical moments, perhaps right in the middle of playing your biggest salmon of the season. Quality tackle gives pleasure and peace of mind.

I like to use nationally advertised brands, sold by a manufacturer who has a reputation to protect, and is thinking long-term. The company wants its tackle to stand up to the tests of time and use so you will buy it again yourself and recommend it to others. Some ''off-brand'' tackle is marketed for a quick buck. This is not to say that all unbranded tackle is of poor quality. However, you should either know the tackle or know the retailer who sells it to you.

8 | USE A ROD WITH LIMBER TIP AND STIFF BUTT

I use a fibreglass rod between 7½ and 9 feet long. It has a sturdy butt and limber tip. The limber tip gives me that all-

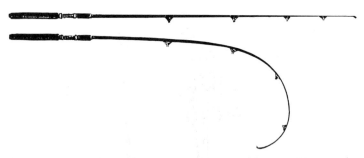

important, shock-absorbing action which keeps a fast-running fish from breaking the line or tearing out the hooks during a sudden lunge. The sturdy butt gives me control when I need it, especially when leading a fish over the net.

Some of my charter customers were light-tackle extremists and would bring light fly rods to test their skill. After hooking a good salmon they would enjoy 10 to 15 minutes of exciting action, then the fish would lie exhausted about 20 feet from the boat. Their light fly rods did not have enough strength in the butt to pull the exhausted fish to the net.

As a result, we would spend another 10 to 15 minutes trying to work the fish those last few feet while my other charter guests waited patiently for their turn to catch a fish. By the time the fish was in the boat, often the hot fishing was over. In my opinion, it would have been far better to enjoy the fish while he was active, then bring him to net and get on with the fishing. If an angler wishes to test his skill to this extreme, his fishing partners should fully understand the situation and be prepared to be spectators and not participants.

9 SINGLE ACTION REEL GIVES MORE CONTROL

I like single action reels better than the star drag models which use a slipping clutch. Single action reels give complete control of the fish, allowing me to apply varying amounts of drag with the palm of my hand and, more important, allow me to *feel* the fish and enjoy every nuance of the fight.

Star drag reels, on the other hand, rely on the clutch to slow down a running fish. Since each fish behaves differently, the drag adjustment is at best a compromise to handle an "average" fish (whatever that is!).

While a charter guide, I hosted guests who used star drag reels and played their fish with no knowledge or feel of what the fish was doing. They just cranked furiously (and continuously) whether the fish was running out against the drag or coming toward the boat. They knew that, eventually, the exhausted fish would end up beside the boat, ready to be netted. This technique may put fish in the freezer, but the angler loses most of the fun and thrill of the catch. He might just as well put a small motor on the reel and just wait to net the fish.

Worse still, many anglers adjust their clutch drags while playing a fish, often with disastrous results. When a stubborn fish just won't come in, the drag is progressively tightened until the fish is under control. As the straining fish is dragged to the net, he often makes one desperate run for freedom and breaks the line or tears out the hooks before the drag can be loosened.

Slipping clutch reels do have some advantages. Older fishermen or those with arthritic hands sometimes cannot master the alternate winding and palming technique of single action reels, and are more comfortable with star drag reels. These reels also have a multiplying action (one turn of the handle means four turns of the reel), allowing the angler to keep up with a fish running fast toward the boat.

In the hands of a real expert, star drag reels can be set with a loose drag and the angler adds a "thumbing" pressure to control the fish. This gives him some of the advantages of the single action reel, plus the advantage of fast cranking when necessary.

However, reels with slipping clutches are more *mechanical*, more expensive and require more servicing.

10 USE PLENTY OF LINE

I like to put plenty of line on my reel because it is surprising how far a big salmon can run. Fifteen hundred to 2,000 feet of 20-pound test line is about right for a five-inch, single action reel.

Incidentally, I think that 20-pound test line is adequate for playing any salmon. With a flexible rod tip, it is almost impossible to pull hard enough to break this line. It also allows you to get more line on the reel than if using a heavier test, and has less friction in the water because of its smaller diameter.

Be sure to store your fishing reels out of direct sunlight as ultraviolet light will cause nylon line to deteriorate quickly. This is one reason I swap the ends of my line at the end of the first season, and discard it after the second season.

11 CHOOSE THE RIGHT BOAT

Trolling is possible using virtually anything from a canoe or dinghy up to a yacht of 100 feet or more. Most trolling,

however, is done using boats ranging in size from 12-foot cartoppers to 40- or 50-foot cruisers.

Cartopper fishermen usually mount a rod holder on each side of the gunwale and fish two rods, possibly using one downrigger for deep fishing. Larger craft can run four to six rods across the stern, and some use up to four downriggers. (Please check the current fishing regulations in your area for "Gear Restrictions".)

The most important considerations for a good trolling boat are:

• Will it troll at an appropriate speed? Many high-powered, planing hull cruisers cannot be run slowly enough for proper

lure action. This is especially true with a large, single engine. Twin engines can be used to overcome this problem by trolling on one engine while using the "dead" propeller to help slow the boat. Boats with large engines can get slower speeds through use of a small auxiliary outboard.

• Another requirement of a good trolling boat is that it have a smooth-running engine. The head guide at a well-known fishing camp in Rivers Inlet kept a record of the fish caught from each of the boats and found that those with rough engines caught the least fish and those with the "sewing machine smooth" engines were the most productive.

A test in Washington State has also shown that commercial trolling vessels with well-tuned engines caught more fish than those with misses or other noises or rattles.

12 ORGANIZE YOUR TACKLE BOX

When you are out on the water it is invaluable to be able to find the right lure quickly, rather than fumble around in a disorganized mass of miscellaneous lures, line, swivels, etc. This means laying out the lures you are planning to use in a convenient spot. Consult your fishing diary and get the size, type and color of lures most likely to succeed. As a general rule, smaller lures are better for summer fishing when bait fish are relatively small, and larger lures better in the winter or in areas where mature herring gather.

Also, be sure you have such basic fishing tools as a pair of toenail clippers (clippers with a straight cutting face, not concave fingernail clippers), long-nose pliers, toothpicks (for herring strip), fishing knife and a good hook sharpener.

13 PREPARE A CHECK LIST

If you prepare a check list, you are less likely to forget some important item. The check list should include such things as good polarized sunglasses (for reducing glare and seeing bait fish and other marine creatures under water), tide book, marine chart, rods, reels, landing net, downrigger, rod holders and any other items which you will need.

You should also include in your check list such personal items as suntan cream, insect repellent and appropriate clothing and rain gear.

14 CHECK YOUR BOAT

If you have a trailerable boat, you should also have a check list to make sure that it is ready. This would include such details as gas and oil for the motor, spare spark plugs (and other items in case of engine malfunction), life jackets, cushions, rod holders, downriggers, extra lead cannon balls, landing net, fish billy, gaff hook, boat fenders, depth sounder, mooring lines and other related items.

15 DOES IT WORK?

It is wise to check the condition of each item. I have had fishing trips ruined because my depth sounder battery was low or my downrigger wires were frayed.

16 PREPARE YOUR LURES

It is usually a good idea to tie up some of the lures you plan to use and store them in your tackle box or on your rod ahead of time. This saves critical minutes during those magic early morning hours when you want to keep your gear working. You'll probably be more alert and under less pressure if you set up your gear the evening before rather than when out on the water. For instance, if leader lengths for a flasher or dodger are critical, you can take the time to get them exactly right. You can also tie up your herring strip holders with fresh leaders and adjust them properly. And take the time to tie proper knots and test them by putting the hook around a solid object and giving a good hard tug on the line.

I usually leave successful lure combinations from one fishing trip just as they are for the next trip. However, it is important to check the leaders on these rigs for any nicks or frays.

38

You should also inspect the last 10 to 15 feet of your main fishing line for nicks and damage from attaching weights, downrigger clips or for abrasion from the line rubbing against the side of the boat. I make it a regular practice to snip off six to eight feet of my main line before every fishing trip, just to make sure.

It is also a good idea to have an extra rod rigged and ready to go. So, if you lose some gear on a bottom hang-up, you can put out the extra rod and be fishing again immediately. An extra downrigger on board can save even more time if your wire breaks or kinks. The damaged gear can be repaired during a lull in the action and you are back to full preparedness again.

17 HANDY CARDBOARD LINE-HOLDERS

I have found that a small strip of heavy cardboard (approximately 1″ x 6″) is a neat and effective holder for any

lure which requires a leader. I use three-ply cardboard (usually available at liquor stores), with a slot cut in each end. Slide the bead chain swivel through the slot at one end, then wrap the leader around the cardboard and stick the hook in the holder at one end. This little organizing trick has saved me many hours of untangling lures in a disorganized tackle box.

18 PLAN A FISHING STRATEGY

There are always many unknowns during a fishing trip, but many other things will be known the night before and it is these that should be used to plan a fishing strategy. For instance, you will know the tidal conditions from your local tide book, and you should also know which areas are most productive on these tides.

You will also have some idea of the forecast weather by listening to radio and television reports. Many areas have special marine reports which will forecast wind and water condi-

tions. These can be used in finding a calm area to fish. Radio, TV and newspaper reports will also give you information on how the fish are biting in various areas. Some of these reports give extremely valuable information, but others are quite suspect. You will have to determine which ones give accurate information and which ones are designed to promote attendance at the local marina or boat rental.

Newspaper reports are often quite thorough, but tend to be somewhat out of date. Radio reports are often the most accurate, and many radio stations have cruisers on the water to give up-to-date information. All of this can be used to help plan a fishing strategy.

19 A PRIVATE NETWORK

Many anglers who fish in the same area often share information. I make it a practice to call a number of local fishing friends and ask about their recent successes. You may find that your friends have been out on the water that very day and can give you information on your fishing spot, including important details on fishing depth, lure type, trolling speed and even likely time of the bite.

20 PARTY FIRST, PAY LATER

Many anglers stay up late the night before a weekend fishing trip, often consuming copious amounts of liquor. When they get out on the water at 5:30 the next morning, they are often hung over, exhausted from too little sleep and ill-prepared to make those on-the-spot decisions that will make the fishing day a big success. They are also unable to appreciate the joys of being on the water early in the morning. Each of us is issued only one body (our own Rolls Royce) which is designed to last us a lifetime. We need to take good care of it to enjoy our fishing and all other aspects of healthy living.

Chapter 3
Finding the Fish

Obviously the most important job for any fisherman is to find the fish. The greatest expert in the world, using the finest tackle and techniques, will be skunked if the fish aren't there.

21	GET OUT EARLY

Most of us aren't really keen to tumble out of bed in the dark in order to be on the fishing grounds at the crack of dawn, but it usually pays big dividends and is well worth the effort.

That jarring sound of the 4:00 am alarm is just as tough on me as anyone, but once I am up and moving, I love the early morning. I never get over that feeling of wonder at the beauty of dawn and the renewal of life and activity.

COME AN' GET 'EM!!

And there is no question that, all other things being equal, fishing is best during the first two hours of daylight. As far as we know, most fish do not feed at night and so are hungry in early morning. Sometimes fish will migrate during the night and arrive at their new location early in the morning, famished after their long overnight journey.

Bait fish are also on the move early in the morning. The plankton are often at the surface at night and move down as the light brightens. The bait fish will be following them.

I had an interesting conversation with a biologist who worked on a mid-Pacific research team at about the 180th degree longitude. This team was attempting to determine which salmon in the area were heading for Canada and the United States, and which for Japan and the Soviet Union.

This mid-ocean area is unique in that it has no tidal action to speak of. This eliminates the tide change factor which often affects fish-biting patterns along the west coast. With no tide factor, researchers found that over 80 per cent of the salmon were caught within the first two hours after daybreak. This was confirmed by all of the research boats over a long fishing period.

22 FISH THE BACK EDDIES

Back eddies are those places where the tide or current moves around a point of land or other obstruction and forms an area of quiet water behind it. These spots are often good holding areas for salmon which, like all fish, are basically lazy and don't

want to work hard fighting a current. (In a way it's similar to stream fishing where the most lucrative waters are often behind a big boulder or other quiet spot in an otherwise rushing current.)

Plankton are swept into these back eddies and attract the euphausid shrimps, herring and bait fish. This makes back eddies even more attractive for salmon and other game fish.

23 FISH TIDE LINES

Tide lines or places with surface debris are often areas of mixing currents and are favored by salmon which usually lie on the quieter side of the tide line. Plankton and bait fish also gather here, sometimes hiding under floating logs or weeds. Migrating salmon will often follow these tide lines even when they are far away from shore on their route to the spawning rivers.

One morning I was fishing for big, mature chinooks, close to a favorite shoreline near Cowichan Bay on Vancouver Island. I watched in surprise as another boat, more than 100 yards from shore, hooked and landed a beautiful 30-pounder. I couldn't understand why that fish was so far from shore until I noticed a slight tide line moving out from a nearby point, pushed by a strong flooding tide. Following my "keep flexible" rule (Secret 6), I started working that tide line in earnest and was rewarded with a fat chinook within half an hour.

24 WATCH THE GULLS

Seagulls flying high above the water are like aerial spotter planes which can see the salmon and bait fish far better than we can from the water's surface. When you see them hovering above a certain area or dipping down into the water, it usually means they are near some fish.

When they gather in great flocks, squawking and squealing and diving into the water, they have found a bonanza and the salmon are often underneath pushing bait fish to the surface.

LET'S CIRCLE HERE A WHILE, AND LURE THOSE GUYS AWAY FROM OUR FAVORITE FISH SPOT...

25 DIVING BIRDS TELL SECRETS TOO

Diving sea birds (often erroneously called diving ducks) are also an excellent sign of salmon. In fact, diving birds are often a more dependable indicator of salmon than seagulls.

My own experience is that murres, murrelets and rhinoceroses auklets (easily identified by the distinctive hump on their beak) are the most reliable indicators of concentrations of bait fish and salmon. Grebes, cormorants and others often turn out to be false alarms for me, but I know others who feel they are good indicators of fish.

Diving birds can also give you some tip-offs regarding the type of bait to use. Sometimes you will see them with the actual bait fish in their mouths. You can see if they are feeding on needlefish or on herring and get an idea of the approximate size of bait for matching against your own lure. You'll find that a pair of binoculars is helpful for studying diving birds.

We have some dramatic underwater footage of murres attacking herring in Juan de Fuca Strait. The murres swim down under the herring, always attacking from the bottom so that the herring are held trapped at the surface. They also "herd" the edges of the school like cowboys at an annual roundup.

Sometimes, however, it is only the birds which are feeding on bait fish and there are no salmon in sight. But even if salmon are not evident, it is wise to work the surrounding area because non-feeding fish usually stay near the feed, close to their next meal for when they do get hungry.

26 FISH ABRUPT DEPTH CHANGES

Any steeply shelving area, whether it is against the shore or a change in depth offshore (near a shallow reef for example) is an excellent holding ground for salmon. Chinooks especially seem to like these areas of abrupt depth changes. Mature, migrating chinook salmon will hug steeply shelving shorelines. I have caught many large chinooks (40 pounds and

up) within 10 to 15 feet of almost vertical rock shorelines. Feeding immature chinooks will also concentrate tight against a bank in many instances.

Weed beds and kelp patches also provide an edge along which salmon will cluster. They will also hide out in the kelp beds, ready to rush out and attack bait fish moving nearby.

27 WORK THE BOTTOM

Many salmon, especially chinooks, seem to hug the bottom, except during active feeding periods or at the crack of dawn or evening twilight. I think that salmon (and all fish) like to be near some sort of reference point, whether it be a shelving shore or the bottom itself. Moreover, the bottom acts as a drag on water current so there is less movement and the salmon does not have to work so hard to maintain its position.

The bottom is also a rich source of food. On sandy bottoms the needlefish (sandlance, candlefish) spend much of their time just above the sand or actually buried in it. Salmon hang close to the bottom in these sandy areas on the lookout for a tasty meal.

Mud bottoms contain sea worms, while rocky bottoms have shrimp and prawns.

28 FISH CLOUDY WATER AND SHADED AREAS

Most fish seem to prefer water which is not "gin" clear and areas which are away from direct sunlight. (This is one of the major problems with our underwater television research,

as it is difficult to find salmon in clear, well-lit underwater environments.)

Sometimes where a muddy, freshwater river pours out over a saltwater estuary (and if the water is calm with no wave action to mix the fresh and salt water) there will be a definite dividing line between the murky water and the clear salt water beneath. We will often see this on our underwater camera as it drops beneath the turbid layer and bursts into clear water, almost like an aircraft descending from a fog bank.

Salmon often stay in the clear water under the murky surface layer, feeling safe from attack by surface predators. At places like Rivers Inlet in northern B.C., the rivers contain a colloidal suspension of glacial material which cuts visibility to only a few inches. Lowering our underwater camera through this 6- to 10-foot layer, we often poked out into the clear water and saw both pink and chinook salmon in sizable schools just beneath the covering layer.

29 LOOK FOR "ROLLERS" AND "JUMPERS"

This is the surest fish sign of all. You actually see the salmon as they roll on the surface or jump clear of the water.

You can't get any more positive sign that fish are nearby and you should fish these areas intensely.

Many people claim that rollers and jumpers will not strike; perhaps they have had frustrating experiences trolling through a school time and again with no success. And while it is true that rolling and jumping fish are often gathering near spawning areas and are thus less interested in active feeding, they *will* strike under certain conditions. (We will deal with these pre-spawning fish in a later section.)

Another excellent sign is fish "finning" on the surface. These fish are usually active feeders looking for bait fish or feeding on euphausid shrimps.

30 | WATCH FOR LANDING NETS

When the landing net comes out on a nearby boat, you know that someone has solved the mystery of finding the fish. By all means, learn what you can from this situation.

Close observation (with binoculars if possible) can reveal many things to help improve your chances of success. Note the size of sinker as the fish is brought in, or look for the downrigger being retrieved to give you clues about depth. Some fishermen will even count turns as the successful angler cranks in his downrigger. Look also for the size and type of flasher or dodger and the size and color of the lure in the fish's mouth as it is brought on board.

You can also watch the boat as it begins fishing again; observe its trolling speed and the area on which it concentrates. You can also watch the line being let out for additional clues on lure type and depth.

31 ASK OTHER FISHERMEN

Of course the most direct method is to just ask the successful fisherman for all the details. When I made this remark at one of my fishing classes, a voice from the audience shouted, ''Yeah, and they'll lie like hell!'' Sometimes they will, but I find that most fishermen are willing to share information if approached tactfully.

After the fish has been landed, I often troll over to the successful crew and congratulate them on their success and ask about the size of the fish. Usually they are delighted to talk about their fish and will often hold it up for me to admire.

I then follow up with questions on type of lure and fishing depth. These two bits of information, along with the area of catch (which you have observed already) give you enough information on his or her success.

32 LISTEN TO YOUR RADIO

Many fishing boats are equipped with CB or VHF radios. Each fishing area has a preferred channel on which

fishermen exchange information on their catches and on successful locations and lures. Some areas have become so competitive that this information is "coded".

You can also use your radio to ask for information on fishing conditions. I remember one plaintive call from a female angler who "just had to have salmon for relatives who were coming for dinner that night." The response was instantaneous and she got enough tips to fill a whole chapter of this book.

33 A DEPTH SOUNDER IS CRUCIAL

This electronic tool is one of the most valuable any fisherman can have on board. It gives him underwater "eyes" with which to learn about bottom contours, location of salmon and location of schools of bait fish. I have become so dependent on my depth sounder that I once stopped fishing in the middle of a holiday weekend when my sounder quit, rushed back to town, and rousted my repair man from his backyard deck chair to make emergency repairs and get me back on the water.

I use a flasher sounder for tracking the bottom when deep downrigger trolling. It also helps spot concentrations of fish and bait.

Graph sounders give the same information in much greater detail, especially in distinguishing bait fish from salmon, and even distinguishing size and species in some instances.

Some of the new video hydrograph units combine the advantages of flasher sounders (instantaneous readout, no expensive graph paper) with the detail of graph sounders. Some of the more sophisticated models give readouts in color and have memories so you can recall certain readouts for re-examination.

Many anglers have sounders, but do not use them properly. They are sensitive instruments and will not give you accurate information unless properly adjusted. Spend some time reading the instruction booklet and work particularly with the sensitivity controls so you can get enough feedback to get good bottom and fish readings without all the unwanted "static" or "clutter" which can be confusing.

34 TRY A TEMPERATURE PROBE

Great Lakes salmon anglers have used temperature devices for many years. The large freshwater lakes are quite stratified and have a thermocline where temperature change is quite rapid. Often salmon and bait fish are found in this area of

temperature change. Locating it is probably *the* most important factor in Great Lakes salmon fishing.

My own belief was that Pacific coast waters were cool enough and tidal mixing thorough enough that temperature was not a factor here. However, recent tests with temperature probes in conjunction with my underwater camera have convinced me otherwise.

During our underwater experiments we attached a probe to the camera and began to record the temperature when we found salmon. Trolling at our normal depth of 30 to 35 feet, we found salmon at a water temperature of approximately 53°F. One morning we were trolling with no success and found that most of the other boats were also having no luck. Our temperature probe read 55°. We lowered the camera until the temperature dropped to 53° and, almost magically, there were the salmon. They had moved another 20 feet deeper to find the preferred water temperature.

For the rest of the summer we used the temperature probe as our primary method of finding fish. We merely lowered the camera until we reached the 53° range and almost invariably found the salmon as well. We plan further tests to find preferred water temperatures in spring and fall.

Incidentally, biologists tell us that fish will be completely inactive if the water drops below 39°F and any temperature above 55°F will not be comfortable for salmon.

Chapter 4
Between You and the Bottom

Trolling is probably the most popular method of salmon fishing throughout Canada and the United States, including the Great Lakes region of Ontario. Trolling has many advantages. It allows you to cover a great deal of water; exposes your lures to fish in many different areas and gives those lures "action" and/or that life-like or "wounded fish" appearance that entices salmon to strike.

35 | FIND THE RIGHT DEPTH

Getting your lure to a depth where the fish are holding is probably the most important consideration in successful trolling. However, it is often difficult to *know* just how deep your lure is actually running. As you let out your line it goes back in a parabolic arc, with a gradually decreasing angle so the line is most horizontal where it enters the water. The degree of this arc is dependent on many factors, including weight of lure and sinker, size and water resistance of the lure and flasher, line diameter, trolling speed and direction, and tidal condition.

In my opinion, downriggers are by far the best method to get your line down deep, get precision depth control and still be able to play and land the fish on light tackle without dragging heavy weights or gear along with the running fish. Downriggers accomplish the latter task very well, but the following will also help provide more depth per ounce of weight.

36 | USE THIN DIAMETER LINE

Thin diameter line creates less drag in the water. The difference between even a 15- and 20-pound line is quite apparent. The 20-pound line (of larger diameter) will keep the line closer to the surface than a 15-pound line with the same weight attached.

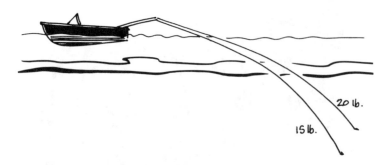

37 | TROLL SLOWLY

This also minimizes drag, but often makes it difficult to get proper lure action. Try wobbling spoons, "flatfish" type lures, or specially rigged herring baits.

38 USE TRIP WEIGHTS

There are a number of gadgets on the market which will allow you to drop a heavy lead weight as soon as a fish strikes. However, this requires a stiff, heavy rod to hold the line while trolling. Drop weights are also expensive to lose each time you get a strike, and sometimes the net result is only a dogfish or a big chunk of seaweed.

39 USE PLANERS

These devices present a perpendicular surface to the line and drag it deep. They trip to a less resistant angle after a strike, but they also require a stiff rod for trolling.

DOWNRIGGERS FOR PRECISE DEPTH

40
A downrigger is simply a large gurdy wheel holding 200 feet or more of wire line which is attached to a short rod extending over the side of the boat. A seven- to ten-pound lead weight drags the wire line to the desired depth, and a fishing line clipped to the wire line trips free when the fish strikes.

Get a good downrigger with an easy-to-read counter so you can measure fishing depth at all times. Using a downrigger with a depth sounder can be a deadly combination.

As mentioned earlier, salmon are often found close to the bottom and sometimes will take only lures trolled within a few feet of the bottom. By watching your depth sounder, you can crank the downrigger up and down over bottom contours, keeping your lure right in the strike zone at all times.

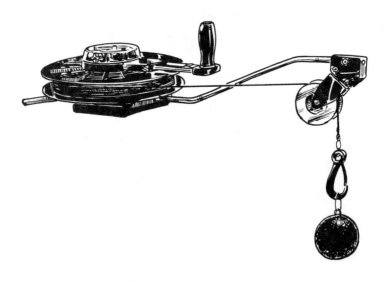

DOWNRIGGERS FIND "FISHY" DEPTHS

41
I often use two lines on each downrigger. This allows me to cover up to four depths at once while seeking out the productive fishing grounds.

I will often continue to change depths on both downriggers, sometimes covering the whole spectrum down to 200 feet. Once the productive depth is found, the extra lines can be removed and both downriggers targeted to catch fish.

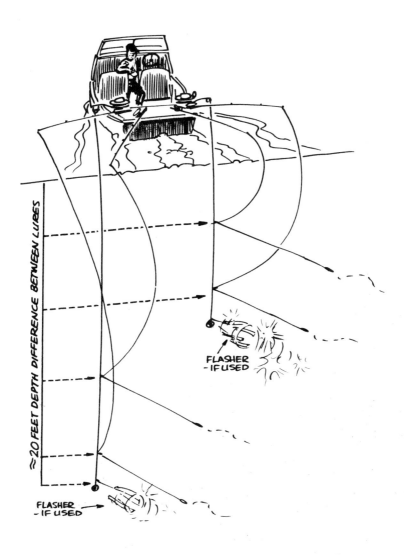

≈ 20 FEET DEPTH DIFFERENCE BETWEEN LURES

FLASHER
- IF USED

FLASHER
- IF USED

42 FLASH UP YOUR DOWNRIGGER

I dislike using flashers and dodgers as part of my fishing tackle because, in my opinion, it takes a great deal of the sport out of playing a fish. There is no doubt, however, that flashers and dodgers are effective in attracting fish, so I use a fishing technique that provides the benefits without the problems of dragging hardware on the fishing line itself. What I do is hook my flasher or dodger on a four to five foot, 80-pound nylon leader and attach it just above the downrigger weight with a bead chain snap swivel. The flasher then rotates in the water (with no lure attached) and puts out an attracting flash and thumping vibration which brings fish to the area. We found that almost five times as many fish came to look at our underwater camera when we used a flasher as an attractor than when we did not.

We have also experimented with various forms of gang trolls (such as lake trolls, ford fenders and other trout gear) as attractors, and these also work, but not nearly as well as a big rotating flasher.

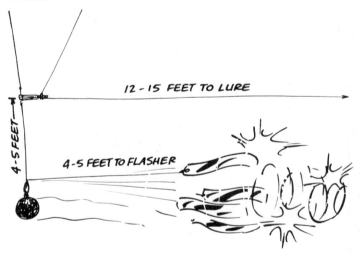

Our fish behavior studies, using a flasher and lure in the conventional arrangement, indicated that salmon sometimes were shy about approaching too close to a flasher. This was especially true of large chinooks which would sometimes cruise back and forth behind the lure and flasher, but would not approach to strike. Indeed, both commercial and sport fishermen have found that they have greater success on big fish with long leaders (often five feet or more) between flasher and lure, a fact which tends to confirm our findings. Using a flasher on a separate line attached to the downrigger will help overcome this problem.

43 | KEEP TENSION ON DOWNRIGGER WIRE

Downrigger wire carries an expensive cargo. The seven- to ten-pound cannon ball, snap swivel, flasher attachment and release clip can all add up to $15 or $20. Maintaining the wire in good condition will prevent loss.

The single most important way to protect downrigger wire is to keep some tension on it at all times. Never allow downrigger wire to go slack, even when it's stored on board the boat. I keep my cannon ball hooked on the downrigger even when mounting or dismounting it from the gunwale bracket and never lift the weight into the boat with slack line hanging over the side. Slack wire tends to twist on itself and a serious kink will result when the line is tightened. When storing my downrigger I wind the line tight to the pulley and hook the snap swivel back around the wire to hold it tight while in storage.

One more tip — never drop your lead weight over the side on a slack wire. If you do, you will instantly learn one of the basic laws of physics: The momentum of a free-falling lead ball will snap the wire or snap-swivel after only a short drop.

TAKE CARE OF YOUR DOWNRIGGER WIRE

44   If you get a kink or broken strands in the wire, it should be cut and re-spliced immediately. This is a relatively simple procedure and will make the wire as strong as new. Get some good wire cutters and crimping tools to do this job properly. Most sporting goods stores should carry them. If your downrigger wire breaks at the crimping sleeve, it means that you have squeezed the crimps too tightly.

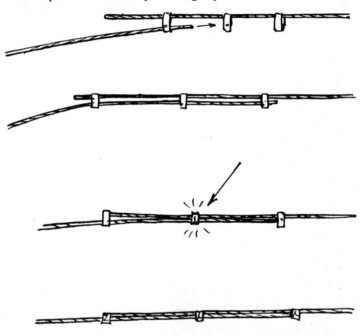

Despite careful use, downrigger wires will develop a tendency to twist. This can be eliminated if you take time to untwist the wire at the end of each fishing trip. Simply put a light lead weight (perhaps one pound) on the snap swivel at the end of the downrigger wire and troll it in deep water. This will allow the line to relieve itself of any strain and twist.

Incidentally, downrigger wire can be stressed by being pulled over too small a pulley at the end of the downrigger arm. The larger the diameter of this pulley, the less stress on the downrigger wire itself. Keep this in mind when deciding which unit to purchase.

All downrigger wire is made of stainless steel, but it does seem to pick up rust spots from repeated intermittent exposure to salt water. There are many grades of stainless steel, and

apparently downrigger wire is not quite as "stainless" as it could be. You can minimize the damage caused through saltwater exposure by periodic applications of a rust preventative such as WD-40 which will drive out moisture trapped in the wire and protect and lubricate it.

45 ROUND WEIGHTS BEST

Downrigger fishing originated in the Great Lakes area of the United States and most downriggers developed there

come with fancy streamlined weights with release clips attached right to the weight itself. These weights are pretty flashy looking and probably have a lot of sales appeal, but, in my opinion, they are not as good as a simple round ball. The whole idea is to get as much depth per ounce of weight as possible, a feat best accomplished by exposing the *minimum* surface area to the water, thereby reducing the friction drag which keeps the weight from reaching maximum depth.

Basic physics tells us that a sphere or ball-shaped weight will enclose the most weight in the least surface area. This means that it is the most efficient and, luckily, only about half as expensive as some of the fancy streamlined weights.

(SAME LENGTH OF LINE)

I tested this theory near my home at Patricia Bay on Vancouver Island. I lowered two downrigger weights of identical poundage (one round, one streamlined) to an exact depth of 100 feet, then trolled from deep water onto a sandy shelf. Inevitably the round ball hit bottom first, meaning, of course, that it was trolling deeper than the streamlined Great Lakes weight.

Some advocates of streamlined weights say that round balls will spin and cause the wire line to twist. Sometimes this is true, but the spin can be stopped by simply adding a "pigtail" to the downrigger ball. To do this, drill a small hole into the side of the ball and insert about 10 inches of ¼-inch polypropylene line secure it with some one-inch galvanized nails. This will keep the ball from spinning and is also handy for lifting it on board.

46 | AVOID BOTTOM HANGUPS

One thing you will learn very quickly when using downriggers is that bottom hangups can come suddenly, unexpectedly . . . and can be very expensive. Indeed, learning to fish with downriggers is somewhat like learning to drive a car: In that regard, I remember concentrating so much on co-ordinating my hand and foot pedal movement that I sometimes forgot to watch where I was going. In the same way, getting used to co-ordinating downriggers, lures, fishing rods and rod holders often means that you forget to watch the depth sounder or where the boat is heading. This will likely result in a few bottom hangups and lost tackle before good old trial-and-error teaches you to be more alert.

It is a good idea to learn basic downrigger techniques over a sand or mud bottom. This allows you to hit bottom without losing any tackle. Sometimes you will gather up some seaweed and debris, but at least the gear will come back more or less intact. Rocky bottoms are a different story entirely.

The only way to avoid bottom hangups is to know the water thoroughly, use marine charts and — most important — use a good depth sounder. Keep it turned on all the time you are fishing and monitor it continuously.

You can also use shore markers or "gun sight marks" to plot your direction of travel. For instance, you can keep yourself on course along the edge of a drop-off by lining up an object on shore with another object farther inland. This will give you an exact line to follow.

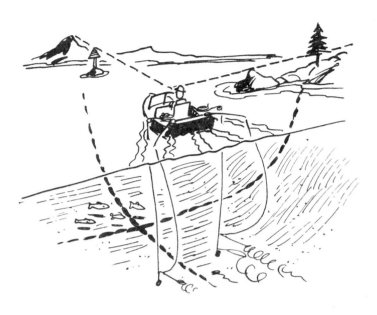

An "anti-snag" device on your downrigger weight will also warn you of imminent contact with the bottom. This is simply a piece of stiff wire (coat hanger wire or heavier) which is attached to the downrigger ball (or actually inserted in a hole drilled in the weight) and extends below it. When the wire hits bottom it telegraphs a signal to the surface warning you to raise the weight — quickly. It works much like the spring devices attached to car fenders to indicate when you are getting too close to the curb.

47 HANDLING BOTTOM HANGUPS

Despite the precautions listed above, sooner or later everyone will get caught on a bottom hangup. The procedure for handling this situation will vary according to the prevalent tide and wind conditions. For instance, if you are fishing in a relatively quiet area with little tidal movement and no wind, you can simply put the boat in neutral and reverse or circle around to work the weight free of the bottom. In this situation it is usually best to trip the fishing lines and reel them in as quickly as possible (as well as any other downriggers which are not hung up on the bottom). Otherwise, stopping the boat will allow the rest of the gear to settle on the bottom, resulting in even more hangups.

The more common situation occurs when there is some tidal movement and/or some wind which makes it more difficult to stop or change boat direction fast enough to free the weight quickly. When the weight hits a rocky bottom, I find it best to jerk hard on the downrigger crank in an effort to jolt the weight loose, rather than "baby" the weight by loosening the gurdy. Loosening the line often allows the weight to settle deeper into a rocky crevice, making it almost impossible to work loose, especially against a wind or tide. Jerking the weight hard will sometimes cost you the lead (the snap swivel opens to release the trapped weight), but it will usually save the rest of the gear. Trying to work it loose will often result in losing flasher, lure, release clip and often a good chunk of downrigger wire to boot.

By keeping a close watch on the downrigger wire, you can react immediately upon hitting bottom and pull the weight free in most instances.

48 | SET DOWNRIGGER LINES PROPERLY

To minimize tangling, a definite procedure should be followed in putting out downrigger lines. The boat should be moving in a straight line at trolling speed. (Try to anticipate movement of other boats so you won't have to turn unexpectedly in the middle of putting out the gear.) Lower the downrigger ball into the water, then strip out 15 to 20 feet of line from the reel and attach the line to the release clip. Check lure action to make sure that it is working properly. Snap the release clip onto the downrigger wire and lower away.

If you are using two lines on one downrigger, lower the gear to the second set of line markers and repeat the procedure for the second fishing line before lowering to the desired fishing depth. It is desirable to have a downrigger with a clutch-brake system which allows a smooth, easy lowering of the gear and saves half the work. You don't have to crank it down as well as up. When turning the boat you must be careful that the downrigger wire does not catch in the propeller. This can become more of a problem when using a small auxiliary outboard on one side of the stern, since only a small turning angle will bring the wire close to the propeller. A stiff wind from the side or fishing in a cross-tide can cause the same problem, forcing the downrigger wire under the boat and toward the propeller. One way to counter this situation is simply to reach over the side with a gaff or boat hook and lift the wire clear of the propeller.

Sharp 180° turns should also be avoided, especially when using multiple downriggers in deep water. Downrigger wires can wrap around themselves in this situation and become a real mess to untangle. I remember fishing a big tide-rip in Sansum Narrows when we got our downrigger wires twisted together under the boat, a mess which took almost an hour to untangle. We lost one downrigger ball and, more important, missed the best fishing of the day.

49 | WATCH DOWNRIGGER PULLEY, NOT ROD TIP

Since your fishing rod is attached firmly to a release clip on the downrigger wire, any fish strike is transmitted immediately up the wire to the downrigger pulley. In fact, the downrigger pulley is a more reliable indication of a strike than the rod tip itself.

The line between the rod and the release clip is subject to fouling with weed and also has a strong friction drag which changes as it passes through the propeller wake or a tide line. These influences can often give false indications of strikes, causing the rod tip to bounce under the effects of these false alarms. It is much better to watch the end of the downrigger pulley for that telltale jiggle (or resounding thump) which indicates a strike.

Even the tiniest fish will give a few good tugs before giving up and just trailing along on the lure. If you are watching the wire at all times you will see this movement and be able to remove the fish. Otherwise, you might drag the little thing around for hours, drowning the fish and eliminating any possibility of a bigger strike.

50 HAND HOLD WIRE OR USE ALARM BELL

I often sit on the gunwale of the boat, holding the downrigger wire between my fingers while watching the other downrigger on the opposite side of the boat. I sense the slightest strike through my fingers and I seldom miss one using this procedure. If I have several fishermen aboard I often assign each one to hold a downrigger wire.

Some anglers have designed alarm bells which they attach to the end of their downrigger pulley arms. These alarms come in various configurations, but most use an extension arm which magnifies any movement of the downrigger pulley and gives more action to the bell on the end. Some of these bells work very well, but others ring all day long, making them useless for detecting strikes as well as driving the fisherman crazy with the noise.

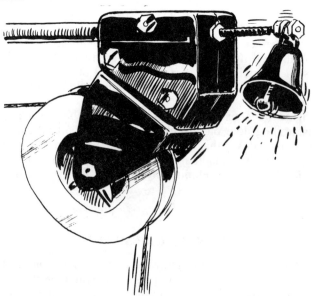

Chapter 5
Trolling Techniques

I believe that trolling with a downrigger is *the* most effective trolling technique and I use this method 90 per cent of the time. The only exception is when trolling bucktail flies on the surface for coho salmon. This is probably the most exciting and sporting way to catch salmon, but surface-feeding coho are only available for short periods during the season.

The following trolling techniques can be used with or without downriggers since the same general principles apply.

51 | CHOOSING THE RIGHT LURE

A group of anglers working a school of fish can usually catch them on a number of different lures, but some general principles apply no matter what they use. Note the following:

• Match the size and shape of natural bait in the area. Fish are

more easily tempted into striking if your lure looks like the natural feed they are trying to catch. They are conditioned to seek out the wounded bait fish, so the more your lure looks like that particular bait fish, the more likely the strike.

• Small spoons such as Point Defiance, Kripple K and Tom Mack match the general shape of herring. (The spoon should get larger as the season progresses to match the bait's growth.)

Long, narrow spoons, bucktail flies and thin hoochies match the needlefish or sandlance which are usually found over sandy bottom areas. Hoochies and bucktail flies also imitate squid which are found in open waters off the coast; they can also be used to simulate shrimp.

• One more tip regarding spoons is that almost any type can be made much more effective by adding a tiny bit of bait to the trailing hook. This can be tiny indeed, perhaps only 1/16th of an inch wide by ½-inch long. If this bit of bait dampens lure action, use a piece of skin or even a tiny piece of plastic hoochie tail to give added action.

52 | LARGE BAITS CATCH TROPHY FISH

A major exception to the above is when fishing for trophy-sized salmon. Our underwater television tests showed quite conclusively that large salmon preferred a large bait, even when the natural feed in the area was small. Moreover, biologists tell us that this ties in with a ''conservation of energy'' habit practised by large predators of many species of fish and animals. Salmon become lazier and wiser as they grow larger. They don't want to use a lot of energy chasing small bait when they can gulp down one large one.

HURRY UP! I'M REALLY HUNGRY!!

This brings to mind an interesting and illuminating experience I had while visiting New Zealand with my family during a once-in-a-lifetime South Pacific holiday. We chartered a fishing boat skippered by one of the top guides in New Zealand's Bay of Islands. This guide had more than 40 years experience, including some time as a crew member on the boat used by Zane Grey on his famous fishing trips many years ago. The guide told us that New Zealand marlin were not large; the biggest he had ever caught weighed some 275 pounds.

Before fishing we jigged some Kawai as bait. These tuna-like fish averaged about two pounds, and the boys really enjoyed catching them. Suddenly Kevin hooked and landed a huge eight pound specimen which the guide wanted to throw back. Kevin insisted that we keep it; it was the largest of the day, so we threw it into the bait tank with the others.

Later we ran into a school of hammerhead sharks and they gobbled all of our bait. The guide told us we should go to artificial lures. I suggested we try the eight pound Kawai still in the bait tank. He chuckled and said that they *never* used bait even half that large. However, I insisted, so he rigged the bait and trolled it over the stern. Within 20 minutes we hooked a huge marlin, battling it for several hours. It weighed over 400 pounds and won the award for the largest marlin taken in New Zealand waters that year.

I believe that our success was more than luck. We were using bait two or three times as large as that used by any other boat in the area and that grandfather marlin knew what he wanted.

53 ATTACH THE LURE CORRECTLY

Most quality lures are designed with great care to give superior fish-catching action when trolled properly. One of the most important details in this regard is balance. Your leader should be tied directly to the lure itself to maintain the balance designed into the lure by the manufacturer.

78

You should never hook a snap swivel or other device to the leading edge of the lure because this could completely alter its balance and action. It may be a bit more convenient to hook lures this way, but you are defeating the whole purpose. You can, however, use a snap swivel between the leader and main line. I use a bead chain snap swivel at the end of my main line and hook another swivel to the end of my leader. This allows me to change lures quickly when leaders are already attached to them.

The action of a plug can also be changed dramatically by the position of a knot tied to the eye in front of the lure. Tying the knot snug at the top of the eye will make the lure dig deeper than tying it to the center or bottom of the eye. Many expert plug fishermen use knot positions as a major adjustment in controlling plug action.

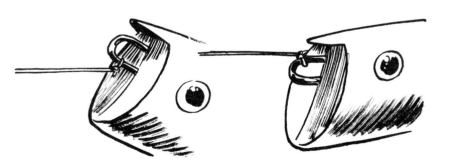

TIE A GOOD KNOT

More fish are lost because of poor knots than for almost any other reason. Some anglers just don't know how to tie a good knot and others are just too careless to do it properly.

Several manufacturers of monofilament line have their own knots which they recommend for their particular brand. However, most knots are a variation of the jam knot, blood knot or clinch knot. This last knot is tied by wrapping the line around itself several times and then looping it back through the gap between the hook and the first loop.

The following illustration shows two of the knots I like best:

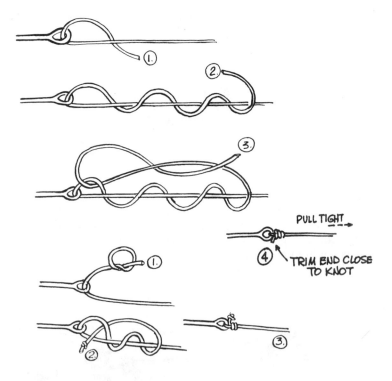

LUBRICATE LINE BEFORE TIGHTENING KNOTS

55

Nylon line can score, burn or fray when pulled tight. It is important to wet the line (with a bit of saliva) before pulling the knot tight. This lubricates the line and cools it a bit, minimizing the scoring problem.

56 CHECK LURE ACTION

This simple tip seems so obvious, but it is amazing how many fishermen are so eager to get their lure in the water that they just throw it over the side and strip out line without bothering to see whether it is working properly.

What is proper action? Most lure manufacturers have detailed instructions enclosed in their packages and usually give tips on proper action for each lure. By all means read these instructions thoroughly and take advantage of a manufacturer's research and experience. After all, he is successful only if you catch fish, and his instructions should give you the best possible information.

Checking lure action beside the boat will also make you aware when an *unusual* action turns out to be productive. Sometimes I have been unable to get my herring strip working "normally", but have lowered it down anyway rather than change to a fresh bait. Sometimes I am startled by a vicious strike almost immediately. Remembering the unusual lure action, I duplicated it, and have learned a whole new fishing secret for myself.

57 CHOOSE LIKELY DEPTHS

We have covered this point pretty thoroughly in our section on downriggers, but for non-downrigger trollers there are two other basic patterns to consider:

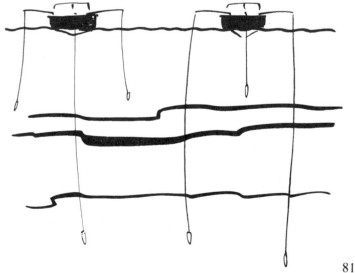

- If you expect the fish to be at shallow depths, put two shallow lines on each side of the boat and a deep line down the middle.
- If you expect the fish to be deep, hang two deep lines over the side of the boat and a shallow line down the middle.

When fishing with downriggers I will often put a single light line right over the stern to pick up any shallow feeders, especially any coho which might be investigating the propeller wash.

Be sure to count the pulls as you let out your line. (A "pull" is usually about 18 inches and is done by grasping the line at the reel and pulling toward the first rod guide.) If you catch a fish at 40 pulls, you can return to the same depth just as you would with downriggers, although the pull method is not quite as accurate.

58 CHECK YOUR GEAR REGULARLY

I make it a practice to inspect my lures every 15 minutes to one-half hour, whether I am getting strikes or not. This allows me to check that my lures are not fouled with weed or jellyfish. It also exposes the lures to fish in the complete column of water, from the surface to the deepest fishing line. Often a salmon will grab the lure as it is being reeled in or let out.

If I get a strike when bringing in the line I will often fish shallower or faster, since this could indicate a shallow fish or a fish which simply wanted to chase a faster moving lure.

Of course the opposite is true too and if you get a strike when lowering your tackle, this may mean that the fish like a slower moving lure and your trolling speed can be adjusted accordingly.

59 FOLLOW THE FISH DOWN

At the crack of dawn salmon are often feeding very close to the surface, usually on bait fish which are feeding on surface plankton. As the sun moves higher in the sky, the plankton, bait fish and salmon tend to move deeper.

While fish tend to feed more actively in the first two hours after daybreak, they will often bite well into the day if you are willing to follow them deep enough.

I will often encounter a good early morning bite on top of a 50-foot shelf near my home in Saanich Inlet. When the ''bite'' goes dead I usually move offshore to the adjacent deeper water where I will find that the fish are often still in a striking mood.

I can remember one occasion when I had four fishing students on board and we caught four nice salmon on top of the shelf. We continued to follow the fish down the edge of the shelf, lowering our downriggers deeper and deeper. We caught our limit of 20 salmon that morning, most of them over 100 feet down, and the last one (a lovely 14 pounder) was taken just before noon with the downrigger depth counter reading 275 feet. Incidentally, that fish swam straight to the surface (my fishing student could hardly reel in fast enough) and put up a spectacular fight on the surface. Salmon must have a marvelous internal mechanism to adjust to such tremendous changes in pressure.

60 FISH A ZIGZAG PATTERN

Watching salmon follow lures behind our underwater camera, we discovered that they will sometimes follow the lure for long periods without striking. Changing direction, however, will sometimes trigger a strike and indeed, many anglers comment that they often get strikes while making a turn.

Fisheries Department tests off the west coast of Vancouver

Island used commercial trollers to find ways to increase productivity. One of their most significant findings was that catches were higher when boats fished a zigzag pattern as opposed to those that trolled in a straight line.

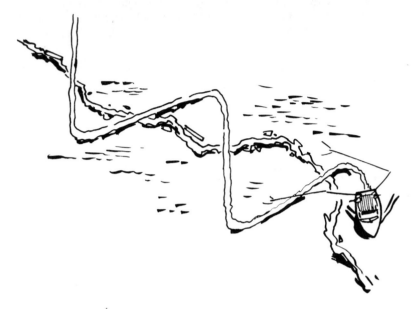

I will often fish along a tide line where two opposing currents mix, usually fishing back and forth across this dividing line with considerable success.

When fishing bucktail flies, I will make very sharp turns of up to 90°. I troll straight ahead for perhaps 100 yards, then turn the wheel hard over to make a sharp change in direction. This causes the outside fly to whip ahead quickly and the inside fly to stop dead in the water. Often these dramatic changes will trigger an excited coho into a smashing strike.

61 | FISH IN ONE DIRECTION

Most fishermen don't know about the important changes in lure action (with relation to tide or wind) that take place when they change direction. Our underwater camera revealed some interesting findings. For instance, trolling with the tide, our lures would often speed up as we went deeper. This is because the surface water moves faster than deeper water, pushing the boat ahead faster relative to the lure.

The opposite happened when we trolled against the tide. We often had to advance the throttle two or three times as fast as anticipated in order to keep the same trolling action on the lures. Sometimes 500 revs on the motor worked with the tide, but we would have to go to 1200 or 1500 revs to get the same action against the tide.

Without access to a camera it would be virtually impossible to get the same lure action in both directions. And even if you do, the fish will still often strike only while you're trolling in one direction.

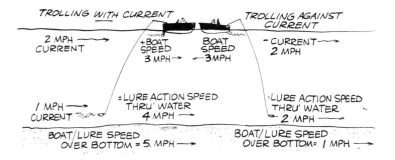

If you get strikes trolling in one direction (usually with the tide), it is usually best not to try to troll back against the tide. Just pull in the gear and run back to the starting point.

62 DOWN WITH THE TIDE, BACK IN THE EDDY

As described earlier, salmon tend to hang out in back eddies. Thus it is *usually* most productive to fish down with the tide just at the outside edge of the eddy, then around and up with the back-eddying tide so that you have the water pushing you along throughout the whole process. If you fish against the tide (in the opposite direction around the circle), you will be fighting the current all the time and probably end up standing still relative to the bottom. If there are many boats fishing an eddy, they will usually fall into a circular pattern like that described and you will have to follow this pattern anyway to avoid collisions.

63 FISH ACROSS THE TIDE

As mentioned earlier, fishing with and against the tide is often productive, as is fishing in back eddies along the tidal flow direction. However, as mentioned in Secret 6, remaining flexible and trying new things often produces unexpectedly good results. This is sometimes true of fishing across the tide, perpendicular to the direction of flow.

During one of our filming expeditions we were working back and forth along a rocky shoreline with very spotty results. Twenty or 30 other boats were following the same pattern, also with no success. I spotted what looked like a tide line about 300 yards from shore. Rather than haul in the underwater camera and all the other gear, we decided to troll across the tide toward this new location. Much to our surprise, we began to take fish in the intermediate area between the shore and the distant tide line, fishing across the main tidal flow.

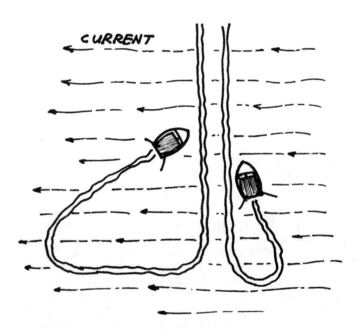

We have repeated this pattern on several occasions and have had good results at least 50 per cent of the time. There seems to be no logical explanation for this except that we were fishing new water untapped by the other boats in the area. Of course, trolling across the tide is only possible in areas where there is not heavy fishing pressure. Otherwise, you will be constantly dodging other boats and their trailing lines.

If you get a strike when fishing across the tide, you should turn into the tidal flow rather than downstream when attempting to get back to the productive spot. An ''upstream'' turn will put you right back where you want to be, while a downstream turn may result in a long struggle to work your way back against the tide.

64 DON'T TROLL INTO THE SUN

Fisheries research describes a test at a trout hatchery which fed its stock with floating food pellets. It was found that the trout always attacked the pellets on the sunny side, often driving all of the pellets to the far side of their pond. This directional striking behavior was most pronounced in early morning or late evening. The trout attacked the pellets with the sun at their back, just like the fighter pilots in World Wars I and II.

After studying this data, we watched our monitors more closely as salmon approached the underwater test lures. We noticed immediately that there *was* a difference in their behavior when we trolled directly toward the sun. They would still approach and follow the lures, but a much smaller percentage actually struck. Often they would strike soon after we made a turn away from the direction of the sun. As with the trout tests, we found this situation most pronounced in early morning and late evening.

We realized that we had often trolled toward the sun during our underwater tests because it put the best light on the lures and on the salmon themselves, giving us better light for our TV pictures. But the salmon obviously couldn't see the lures as well because they had the sun in their eyes. Our underwater camera had discovered another secret which is just plain common sense. Like airplane pilots, and automobile drivers, salmon don't like *steering* into the sun.

65 | USE THE GEAR SHIFT

Mechanics tell me that this technique can be hard on the engine, but it can be effective for certain fishing situations. Once a friend who was having no luck asked me to come along to find out what was wrong. It was obvious that he was trolling too fast, but his high-speed inboard would not troll down. His heavy downrigger weight streamed out behind the boat at quite an angle, robbing him of needed depth and forcing his lures to whirl wildly.

I suggested that we put the motor out of gear and let the downrigger and lures swing down to a more vertical position. Within 15 seconds we were rewarded with a vicious strike and soon after had an eight-pound chinook in the landing net. We used this technique for about two hours and ended up with our limit of 12 nice chinook up to 14 pounds. It took about 45 seconds after putting the motor in neutral for the downrigger to reach a vertical position, then we would put the motor back in gear for two or three minutes until the 150 feet of wire was streaming behind again.

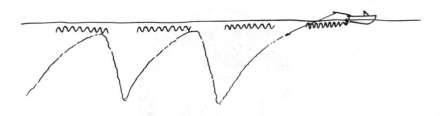

This technique allowed us to troll the lure through a wide range of depths and also changed the lure action. In this instance the fish were very deep and they struck as the lure fluttered down to the bottom of their range, or just after we put the motor back in gear.

You can use the same technique without a downrigger, sometimes getting even more dramatic results. Trolling with six or eight ounces of weight and a long line, the lures will drop down in a long arc between full trolling configuration and vertical. This will cover an even wider range of depths.

66 | VARY YOUR SPEED

Normal trolling speed is the speed at which your lures have the right action. Most lures, however, can be adjusted to give proper action at several different speeds. You can adjust the degree of bend in a spoon, change the knot position on a plug and adjust the hook position on various bait hookups to give proper action at different speeds.

If you are not getting any strikes at your normal trolling speed, speed up 25 to 50 per cent and adjust the lures to work correctly at this speed. You may be surprised at the results. Commercial trollers move much faster than most sport boats and have consistent success because their lures are "tuned" for these faster speeds. Faster speeds also allow you to cover more water, thereby exposing your lures to more fish.

I recall one mid-October morning when we fished for coho in Cowichan Bay on Vancouver Island. Coho were jumping all

over the bay, but none of the 75 boats there were having any success at all. Knowing that coho sometimes like a very fast lure, I decided to test my faster trolling theory to the extreme. I advanced the throttle until the bow of the boat actually began to rise up toward a planing position. Just as I was beginning to feel ridiculous, one of my rods snapped back with a force that almost jerked it clear of the rod holder. The reel screamed at an adrenalin-pumping pitch I have never heard before or have since. After a spectacular fight, we landed a beautiful 12-pound, hook-nosed fish that must have had a twisted neck from the force of the strike.

It can also be productive to troll much slower than normal. This is especially true in areas where chinook salmon are "holed up" and not feeding actively. In this situation it is important to give the fish the maximum time to look over your bait as it wobbles or rolls slowly past its nose.

As a general rule, I like to troll relatively slowly during periods when the fish are not feeding actively, but speed up considerably during the "bite" (when they are actively seeking food). A hungry fish will be triggered by a fast moving bait, while a fish which is resting or digesting its food is not likely to be motivated to chase it.

67 VARY LINE LENGTH

Normally I put my lure about 12 to 15 feet back from my downrigger wire, but sometimes I will put it as much as 20 to

40 feet back, especially if trolling in relatively shallow water. In clear water you can put the lure farther back, and shallow lines can also be back farther to get them away from the boat and propeller disturbance.

If the water is murky, I want the lure to be relatively close to the flasher (rotating on its own line at the downrigger ball) because the fish will be attracted to the vibrating thump but won't see the lure if it is too far away. You can put the lure as close as six or seven feet from the release clip in this situation.

When fishing without downriggers — and especially when using surface-running bucktails — both extremes work well. I often troll my bucktails only 20 to 30 feet behind the boat, and somtimes right in the prop wash where coho are attracted by the bubbles. This is most effective in areas where the coho are still feeding actively.

In estuary areas on the other hand, the fish are sometimes more spooky and won't come near the boat. One morning off Cherry Point near Cowichan Bay we saw one boat take three fish in a row while the other 50 boats were catching nothing but eel grass. I pulled alongside and asked all the usual questions about lure, size and color, but as it turned out we were already doing all of these things correctly. Only as we pulled away and watched him strip out line did we realize that he was fishing almost 200 feet back from his boat, while we were only 60 feet back. Obviously, the fish were extremely wary of all the boat activity. When we matched his long line, we began taking fish almost immediately.

68 USE GUNSIGHT MARKS TO PINPOINT LOCATION

Salmon are often found in tightly bunched schools covering an area of perhaps 50 feet in radius. This is a tiny segment in the vastness of most fishing areas.

Once you locate the fish, by all means mark the spot as precisely as possible. Most "high liner" fishermen use range markers or "gun sight" marks to pinpoint their location. In the excitement of a strike it's often difficult to remember your position, but taking good marks can pay big dividends in getting back to the hot spot.

Most weekend fishermen believe that it is good enough to look toward an approximate shore location or try to line themselves up between two markers on opposite shores. Neither of these methods is very accurate since a 10° error in either direction can put you as much as 900 feet off the correct spot even if you are only ½-mile offshore.

The correct method is to line up two objects on the same side of the boat, one behind the other (a rock on the shoreline with a tall tree behind, for example). Lining up two sets of range markers at approximately 90° to each other will give you two intersecting "lines" and a position exactly over the spot where you hooked the fish.

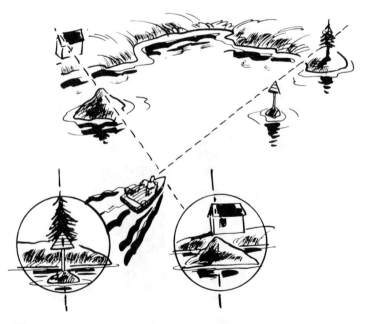

Your first attempts at fixing these marks will probably be awkward and inaccurate, but it is amazing how quickly you will learn to take good marks, especially when you reap the rewards of such a procedure.

After marking the spot you will probably want to put the motor in neutral and enjoy playing and landing your fish. You can then circle around, line up one set of marks, then troll until you cross the other set.

Of course, you will also want to locate the fish in the third dimension (depth), so it is important to note the reading on your downrigger before retrieving it. If you were trolling without a downrigger, you will need to remember how much line (the number of pulls) was out.

69 | MARK LOCATION WITH FLOATING OBJECT

An alternate method of marking a location is to throw a floating object over the side immediately after getting a strike. This can be a seat cushion, bleach bottle (preferably with a one-pound weight to minimize wind drift) or any other appropriate floating object. This procedure works well when the water is relatively calm and the floating object is not hidden in wave troughs. It is also effective on surface-feeding coho when the tide is running. The floating object will move with the school as it drifts along in the tide.

I've seen people throw beer bottles or trash to mark a location, but this is just plain littering. Let's do everything we can to maintain our environment and upgrade the image of fishing and fishermen.

70 | FINDING THE BIG SCHOOL

When I was a fishing charter guide in the late 1950s, I was out on the water almost every day, and learned a lot of special tricks to help me stay with the main body of fish as it moved from one location to another. On many occasions I would have several "hot" days, catching limits for the entire party. Sometimes we would "limit-out" for two parties in one day. With four or five persons in each party and a five fish limit, we might take 30 or 40 fish in one day. Then one morning I would return to the same spot and begin catching smaller runt fish or fish with some deformity (usually a torn mouth from a previous hookup or an injury from a seal or other predator). I soon learned that this meant the main school had started to move to another location. The stragglers couldn't keep up and remained behind to pick up the leftovers.

When I began to catch these undersized fish, I would immediately begin to explore anywhere from a few hundred yards to a quarter of a mile in either direction in search of the main body of fish at the next "holding" spot.

71 | SANDY BOTTOM TECHNIQUE

When fishing on a sandy bottom you can use your downrigger effectively to get the lure right on the bottom where salmon are literally picking the bait fish (candlefish, sandlance) right out of the sand. You can accomplish this by using a long, narrow metal spoon such as the Koho Killer, Koho King or Needlefish lure and attaching it 25 to 30 feet back from the downrigger release clip.

Lower the downrigger quickly and smoothly (a good clutch brake handles this well). Jerky, intermittent lowering of the downrigger can cause the leader to foul with the flasher. When the downrigger ball touches bottom, crank up one or two turns and you are ready to fish.

The weight of the metal spoon and the distance behind the release clip allows it to ride just above the sand. You can also add a tiny weight (perhaps ½-ounce) on the main line near the swivel to the leader.

You will need to check your lure frequently since there is a great deal of lettuce weed and other debris on sandy bottoms, and fouled lures don't catch many fish. You should also keep ''probing'' for the bottom by lowering the downrigger every few minutes to check that you are still riding just above the sand. Your depth sounder will help determine when to lower or raise the downrigger weight.

72 BIG CHINOOK PREFER ROCKY SHORELINES

Large chinook salmon often hang out along steeply shelving, rocky shorelines, sometimes right tight against the rocks. They seem to lie in wait like an animal in its lair, ready to ambush passing bait fish.

They won't travel very far to strike a passing lure, so you must get close to the rocks themselves. I have found it effective to troll straight toward the shore or reef and then turn sharply when the sounder warns of the steeply shelving bottom. This will swing your lures into the chinook's territory, often triggering a strike just after making the turn. This is a risky business, however, since you can hang up the downrigger and all the gear if you cut it too close.

These fish seem almost territorial in nature. Several times I have picked up a big chinook along one of these rocky cliffs and then caught nothing more. However, if I return to the same spot a few days later another big one is often there. Perhaps a new "king of the rock pile" moves in to replace the one caught last time around.

73 | THE PERILS OF WEED

Many "hot" fishing areas seem to be the same areas where a great deal of weed and debris collects. This is especially true in back eddies and tide lines where the same forces that sweep in the plankton also bring the seaweed and other debris.

Often you must troll through these areas to get to the best concentrations of fish. Downriggers are helpful in this situation because the downrigger wire will catch most of the weed and prevent it from getting to the lure itself. Another way to keep debris off your fishing line is by putting the rod tip under water as you pass through areas of heavy weed. This catches debris on the rod which can be shaken free when you get back into clean water again.

Chapter 6
Fishing with Bait

Detailed techniques for fishing with bait have been covered quite thoroughly in my book *How to Catch Salmon – Advanced Techniques*, but we will summarize the most important secrets here in this short section.

74 BAIT HOLDERS SCORE WELL

Top anglers can rig trolling baits with no help from a bait holder, but these plastic devices which fit over the front end of the bait do have a number of advantages.

For one, they give dependable bait action. The curve of the holder and its overall configuration give the lure a definite rolling action. (Baits used alone will soften quickly and action can change dramatically so they no longer attract fish.) Bait holders also allow a bait to be used much longer, even after bumping bottom or hitting seaweed or other debris. Natural baits alone cannot stand up to this abuse.

The most popular bait holder in B.C. is the Strip Teaser lures made by Rhys Davis of Sidney, B.C. They include the original Strip Teaser, Super Strip Teaser, Minnow Teaser, Herring Teaser, and Tiny Teaser.

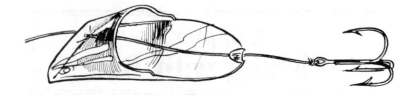

Other bait holders made in B.C. include the Krippled Minnow and Krippled Anchovy made by Jim Gilbert Enterprises, the Spring King lures made by Gordon Robinson of Sooke, the Nosky Killer and others.

Many experienced anglers would argue that bait holders are not necessary, usually because they personally have been so successful using cut-plug herring. Cut-plug herring is simply a piece of herring with its head cut off at an angle so that the remaining portion of the herring body rotates when pulled through the water. This technique can be extremely effective in many situations, but experiments using our underwater camera showed that the salmon preferred whole herring in a Herring Teaser head over cut-plug herring almost four-to-one, even when using the best cut-plugs from top guides.

75 | BEST BAIT ACTION

Our underwater camera revealed that a fast rolling action was most appealing to both coho and chinook in almost every situation. The only exception might be large chinooks near spawning rivers where they will only take bait which literally bumps them on the nose. We don't have underwater pictures of this phenomenon, but it would seem that a slow-moving bait would be more effective in this instance.

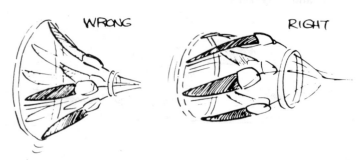

WRONG   RIGHT

It seems that a "tight" rolling action is more effective than a "pinwheel" action where the head of the bait goes in a small circle and the tail in a much larger circle. In any rolling action of the bait it is important that the head of the bait go in the same arc as the tail of the bait.

76 GET GASPING, PULSING ACTION

The tight rolling action described above should also have a beat or pulsing action, like a gasping, twisting, wounded herring which is rolling over but hesitating ever so slightly after each roll as though trying to regain its balance.

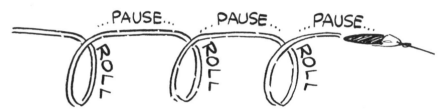

Since each piece of bait is somewhat different in its shape and consistency, setting up and getting an effective bait action is more a case of trial and error than fishing with other lures. It's even difficult to show proper bait action in the two-dimensional, still-action illustrations in this book. A live demonstration in a

water-filled tank or an actual fishing trip is by far the best way to learn.

I used to take all my fishing students on a field trip so we could demonstrate proper lure action and indeed the entire fishing procedure in a real-life situation. It was a wonderful experience for both students and teacher ... we all learned a great deal and inevitably had a beautiful day on the water. Now that my fishing classes average over 200 students, it's impossible to take them all out on the boat, but I'd still love to do so if possible.

77 USING BAITS WITH FLASHERS AND DODGERS

As mentioned earlier, I do not use flashers or dodgers (except on my downrigger) because playing a fish is much more enjoyable without them. However, there is no question that a flasher or dodger will sometimes enhance a bait's action by giving that extra little kick when it may not otherwise be working quite right. Yet, it can also dampen the action and in some cases will scare off salmon, especially big ones which our camera showed tended to shy away.

If you do use flashers or dodgers, it is extremely important to get the bait working well on its own. You can do this by holding a flasher in your hand and putting it in the water with the edge knifing parallel to the water. This will allow the bait to roll normally without the added action of the flasher. You can then make adjustments as necessary before fishing it with the flasher or dodger.

78 TAKE CARE OF BAITS

Herring and anchovy baits are getting extremely expensive, sometimes costing $2 to $3 a package of half a dozen. Herring baits should be kept in a small, insulated bait box with an artificial ice pack on top. Thaw only a few pieces of bait at a time, keeping the rest frozen. This is especially important when using whole herring or anchovy baits, since they soften much faster than strip baits.

Any bait not used can be refrozen. I often refreeze even the herring strips which have already thawed and have actually been used in the water — providing they are still in good shape. I have sometimes refrozen the same bait two or three times without apparent harm to its fish-catching ability.

Another effective method of keeping bait for future use is to salt it. After returning from fishing, place thawed strips or whole baits on a bed of coarse salt and cover them with another layer. This will preserve the baits and also tends to toughen them a bit. Keep them in the refrigerator or a cool place, and they will last at least a week. This method seems especially effective with whole baits, somewhat counteracting their tendency to go soft and mushy.

79 | ADJUST BAIT ACTION

Watching the lure roll beside the boat is important in any trolling situation, but is absolutely vital each time you put out a piece of natural bait. More often than not, I make some adjustment to the bait or bait holder before putting it down each time. Lure action can be modified in the following ways:

• Change hook position. Moving the hook toward the tail of the bait will slow down the rolling action; pulling it forward will speed up the roll. This changes the weight balance of the lure as a whole.
• Change the shape of the bait holder. Plastic bait holders can be twisted by hand to give them more or less bend. (Increasing the bend will speed up the roll.) You can also make more permanent adjustments to bait holders by steaming them over a kettle to get the desired modification. You might even prepare a template to modify all your bait holders if you find a real "killer" action.

MORE ROLL

LESS ROLL

● Modify the bait. Sometimes you can cut off just ¼ inch or ½ inch of the head or the tail of a piece of herring strip to speed up its action. I sometimes trim the tail and cut the meat very thin to improve the action.

With whole herring or anchovy baits you can sometimes alter the action by jamming it tighter into the bait holder, causing a slight weight transfer. You can also adjust the bend in whole-bait by tightening or loosening the hook which is impaling it.

Whole-bait action also changes dramatically depending where the hook is placed in the minnow. The hook can also be inserted into herring strip, but this does hamper some of the natural wiggling action which makes a strip bait so appealing.

Using a larger or heavier hook will slow bait action or speed it up in the case of lighter, smaller hooks. Adding a trailer hook behind the main one will also slow down bait action.

The easiest of the above-mentioned adjustments is the first one — moving the position of the hook — and this is the method I used to use most of the time. However, here again my under-water camera has changed my fishing technique. Since most salmon attack a bait from the tail, I want to get my hook as close to the tail as possible. Finicky feeders also tend to nip lightly at the last ¼ inch of the bait and simply let go unless a hook is right there. This is usually what is happening when you see your rod tip dip back momentarily as though you had a "nibble". Many top experts used to claim dogmatically that this rod tip action was indicative of a salmon slapping the bait with its tail before striking ... until the underwater camera showed otherwise.

So now I adjust my baits by bending the plastic head, cutting the strip itself, or even adjusting boat speed. I do want to keep that hook right at the tail of the bait, and keep it "sticky sharp".

Chapter 7
Mature Salmon in River Mouth Areas

When salmon approach their home rivers and streams, dramatic changes occur, both physically and in behavior patterns. Initially, the salmon begin to darken in color, especially toward the belly. The upper jaw begins to hook over and sometimes both jaws change shape, making the fish into a rather fierce looking beast. Eventually the flesh begins to deteriorate as they move upstream to the spawning grounds.

However, the most important changes to an angler relate to the salmon's apparent lack of interest in feeding. For while they will still strike at lures or baits in certain circumstances, almost

NOT TODAY -- I HAVE A ... ER ... A *HEADACHE!*

all fish caught in river mouth areas have empty stomachs. Obviously, their feeding instinct has been turned off and they are striking for other reasons. Of course their major drive is to get to the spawning grounds to lay eggs and deposit milt in nature's wondrous miracle of the renewal of life. (If reproduction is a once-in-a-lifetime occurrence for salmon, no wonder his attention is focused on it ... tonight's the night!)

80 TROLL SLOWLY FOR RIVER MOUTH CHINOOKS

Big, mature chinooks lying in holding pools near river mouths (or even in the last few miles before arriving at the river) will not chase a bait like an actively feeding fish. However, instinct and a lifetime of voracious feeding might trigger it into striking if we make it especially hard to resist.

We do this by presenting the fish with a lazy, rolling bait or lure which moves slowly through the water. Hopefully, we will be able to troll it close enough to the big chinook so that taking the lure requires no special effort. This is why it is so important to be in exactly the right spot when fishing for mature chinook. If you don't take the lure literally right past its nose, you won't get any action. Usually these holding spots are well known to local fishermen, and many boats (sometimes hundreds) jockey for position over the hot spot. This is why mooching and drift fishing or jigging are often productive in estuaries as anglers try to sit right over the hot spot, keeping their lures working in the holding pool, rather than trolling in and out of it.

81 FISH AGAINST THE BANK

Pre-spawning chinook usually migrate tight against the shoreline, even many miles from their spawning river. Studies show that salmon fingerlings migrate close to the bank on their way downstream, and spawning adults apparently use the same route on the way back. They are sometimes in quite shallow water. I remember hooking one 40-pound chinook while trolling a small aluminum boat under some overhanging trees; my rod bumped into a tree limb as I snapped back the rod to set the hook.

When fish gather at a river mouth they usually lie in a deep pool just at the edge of alluvial silt deposits from the river. As the fresh water mixes with the salt and spreads out into a bay, the water velocity slows and the mud and silt from the river drop to the bottom, forming a shelf against which the salmon lie.

Fishing regulations often prohibit fishing right at the river mouth itself. This is justified (in my opinion) since these big spawners are vulnerable to snagging and other harassment in this confined area. However, if regulations permit, you can sometimes anchor your boat at the top of the silt shelf and drift right over the holding pool.

82 | LEAVE THE CROWDS BEHIND

If a favorite holding area for big chinooks is crowded with boats which have been working it incessantly for several hours, you might try moving a few hundred feet away from the congested area. I think that sometimes big salmon lying in such a pool will move a short distance away to escape the plethora of

lures trolling back and forth through their resting spot. The
vibration from all the motors may also make them uncomforta-
ble enough to move. But after they have settled into their new
spot, there is always the chance that your lure might tempt
them.

83 BE FIRST ON THE WATER

As already mentioned, the first two hours after daybreak are often the most productive for catching fish. This is
especially true in estuaries. Migrating fish often move during the
night and a fresh run of fish could be there waiting for the
early-bird angler. They will have burned up a lot of energy
getting to the holding pool and are more likely to strike than
those that have already settled in. The first lures through the
pool in the morning have an excellent chance of tempting these
fish to strike.

New fish may move into the holding pool at any time of the
day, so it's worth coming back again after a few hours, especially if early morning pressure has been heavy and the boats
have moved to other areas after the morning bite is over. You
can sometimes pick up a fish which has moved in during the lull.

Fishing during tide changes and in late evening can also be productive for the simple reason that the pre-spawning salmon do not shed their lifetime instincts completely and might be tempted to a lure at these traditional feeding times.

84 NATURAL BAITS BEST

All fishing techniques are based on a certain amount of deception, tricking the fish into believing your lure is his natural food. If you are trolling slowly the fish has maximum opportunity to look over your lure. Its natural wariness and a lifetime of successfully avoiding lures makes the wily salmon a pretty tough customer to fool.

While some artificial lures are often productive in river mouth areas, natural bait produces by far the most fish, mainly because it's closest to the real thing. A natural bait trolled inches from a salmon's nose is probably the most difficult for it to resist.

Many anglers use cut-plug herring and mooch it slowly back and forth across the holding pools. Often they cut their baits right on the fishing grounds and discard the herring heads over the side. On at least three occasions I have cleaned large salmon and found these discarded herring heads in their stomachs. One 35 pounder had seven herring heads in its stomach and had probably been sitting down there gulping up the tasty morsels as they drifted past his mouth. Then my rolling Herring Teaser came by and the fish made its big mistake.

85 | PERSISTENCE PAYS OFF

The most popular theory holds that pre-spawners strike because they are irritated by the lure and strike out in anger. I don't think this is their primary motivation, but I think they do in fact strike out at lures for reasons other than feeding.

I recall one beautiful morning on Englishman's River near Parksville on Vancouver Island. I was casting for steelhead trout in a crystal clear pool, gunning in particular for a large steelhead lying at the edge of a riffle. I made at least 100 casts near the fish with the Daredevle lure sometimes passing within a foot of its nose. The steelhead ignored it completely. After casting to several other areas of the pool, I returned for one last crack at the big steelhead. As the lure fluttered past the fish, it suddenly turned and snapped at the lure with a motion that had to be pure anger or frustration. I was so startled I almost let the fish jerk the rod from my hand before recovering to enjoy an adrenalin-pumping battle that only a fresh-run river steelhead can muster.

When crowds of boats continually troll or jig in a confined holding pool, the lures must be almost bumping into the fish time and time again. It seems hard to believe that they wouldn't strike out in frustration at least once in a while.

There is another theory that pre-spawning salmon will strike out in a protective reaction. We know, for instance, that cutthroat trout move up river behind the salmon, often stealing their eggs on the spawning grounds. They have even been known to bump the ripe females in an attempt to dislodge their eggs. This is another reason why large, herring-like baits are effective in estuary areas. The salmon might think it is a cutthroat trout and strike out in an instinctive reaction to protect their eggs.

I sometimes think that it's a shame to harass the salmon in this manner, but there is no question that dogged persistence may sometimes trigger a strike out of frustration or protective instinct.

86 | FISH FAST FOR HOOK-NOSED COHO

River mouth coho can often be taken using the same tactics described above for pre-spawning chinook. In fact, the

world record coho of 31 pounds was taken in Cowichan Bay on Vancouver Island in this manner: Patty Hallberg (wife of Lee Hallberg — the "Old Fisherman" radio commentator) had given up trolling bucktails for coho and decided to go deep and slow-troll for big chinook, when her world record fish struck.

However, successful coho anglers often troll at breakneck speeds with bucktail flies and abalone spinners for big, hook-nosed coho in estuary areas. Trolling Flatfish (U-20 size — orange with black spots is a real killer) or other shovel-nosed lures at accelerated speeds can also bring successful results.

Even drift fishermen who usually find that they get their strikes as their lures flutter to the bottom have found that they can take coho by casting out and retrieving just as fast as they can crank their big, heavy-duty saltwater spinning reels.

Chapter 8
Striking, Playing and Landing a Fish

If you have been studying and putting into practice the tips described thus far, you should already be experiencing one of the greatest thrills in fishing . . . the actual moment of strike. But after going through all of the preparation and development of proper lure techniques, you don't want to miss the big payoff.

87 | SETTING THE HOOK

Salmon will take a lure in a number of different ways and it is important for the angler to set the hook properly in each instance.

Our underwater studies show that more than 80 per cent of salmon attack from the rear, sometimes just nipping at the tail and sometimes completely engulfing the entire lure. As soon as its mouth touches the metal hook, the fish reacts in what looks like pure panic. Its gills fly out, its mouth snaps open and the salmon shakes its head vigorously to get rid of the foreign substance. (He's been eating herring and bait fish all his life and this is the first one that has nipped back. No wonder he's frightened.)

As mentioned earlier, a sticky-sharp hook is the most important thing you can have in preparation for this moment. A hook which is not sharp enough to "stick" will merely skid out of the salmon's mouth. Once the hook sticks, the fish's thrashing will help make it penetrate deeper. If you are fishing with a downrigger and a firmly attached release clip, the hook will often set itself from the force of the fish tripping the release pin. The same is true if you are trolling with heavy weights or are trolling at a fast speed. The heavy weight or fast-moving boat will provide enough resistance to embed the hook.

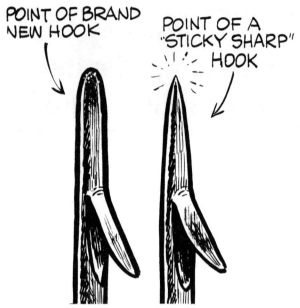

POINT OF BRAND NEW HOOK

POINT OF A "STICKY SHARP" HOOK

However, slower trolling, light-tackle trolling or low-friction downrigger releases need help from the angler to get a solid hook-up. In my opinion, it is best to set the hook on any strike. This insures that the fish is properly hooked before beginning the exciting battle.

If you are fishing with a downrigger or using another technique where there might be some slack in the line, reel in as fast as you can until the line is tight, point the rod at the fish and set the hook by a series of sharp, short, upward tugs, ending with the rod butt pointing back over your shoulder and the tip bowed straight toward the fish. This series of jerks will progressively pull the hook past the barb and make it far more difficult for the fish to throw the hook on any subsequent slack line.

If you are fishing live bait that has small hooks embedded into a swimming bait fish, the salmon will often grab it tentatively and hold it in his jaw for a moment before turning it to swallow the bait headfirst. In this situation it is important to strip a bit of slack line so the fish feels no resistance. Then, when the line begins to move off steadily, set the hook hard.

The same is true with certain slow-trolling techniques using frozen baits or cut-plug herring. If the hooks are well buried in the bait, it is probably best to allow the fish to ingest it fully before driving the hook home.

112

My own preference, however, when using Strip Teaser plastic heads in front of a trolled lure, is to set the hook immediately upon feeling the strike. With my sticky-sharp trailing hooks, the fish usually has the point inside its mouth on the first touch and I want to set the hook before it's spit out.

In downrigger fishing, you can't react fast enough to set the hook because the line must first be released from the downrigger to get a direct pull on the fish. In this case you must wait until the fish is hooked at least enough to pull on the release pin, then finish the job as described above.

88 | KEEP YOUR ROD UP

This piece of advice has been given in almost every fishing book ever written. It is, however, the single most important factor in successfully playing any game fish.

"SHOCK ABSORBER" EFFECT OF ROD FLEXING PROTECTS LINE

NO FLEXIBILITY-- LINE ALONE MUST TRY TO ABSORB PULL OF FISH

The fishing rod is like a giant rubber band or shock-absorber. Holding the butt vertical allows the rod to bend through a full 90° arc, absorbing the sudden runs and lunges of the fish without breaking the line or allowing it to go slack. It gives the angler that extra split-second to wind in or let out line and maintain an even pressure on the fish.

Lowering the rod toward the fish removes this shock-absorber effect and allows no margin of error in handling the reel. Yet it is amazing how many anglers let the rod drop in reaction to a hard run of the fish or as their arms tire after a lengthy fight. I have watched far too many big fish snap the line with a sudden lunge as a tiring angler lowers his rod when the fish nears the boat.

89 LIGHTLY DOES IT

My favorite reels are the single action type which allow me to feel every movement of the fish, and provide complete control of the tension at all times. This is one of the great excitements of fishing, feeling the reel spinning as I palm it and apply a gentle braking action.

I hold the rod above the reel and keep the butt against my hip or abdomen to give me some leverage. As the fish starts to run I feel it instantly with the hand holding the rod and get my fingers off the reel handles to begin the palming action. As my rod hand feels the line tension easing, I reverse the procedure and begin winding in. All of this action becomes automatic with a little practice and the reel hand moves smoothly between reel handles and edge of the spool (for palming). It's almost like playing a musical instrument ... and the music is very sweet.

If you are using a star drag or spinning reel with a slipping clutch, the drag should be set before starting to fish, and left alone during the action. A good way to test the drag setting is to pull line off the reel and watch the rod tip. If the tip remains relatively stable, the drag is smooth, but if it jerks up and down, it is obviously sticking and is probably set too tight.

With a flexible rod tip the drag should be set at only two or three pounds of tension, and perhaps even less if you want to really enjoy playing the fish. I built a special device for testing the amount of bend in a rod at various line tensions. We were amazed to find that an eight- or nine-foot rod with a firm butt and limber tip will be bent double at a pressure well under five pounds.

Setting a light drag on the reel allows you to have at least some of the fun of a single action reel by using your thumb on the spool to apply additional pressure when controlling the fish.

One of the biggest mistakes made with star drag reels is to tighten the drag when a stubborn fish refuses to come toward the boat. The over-tightened drag gives much more control of the fish, but a sudden lunge near the boat will often snap the line before the angler can readjust the drag setting. For this reason, it's far better to use a light drag and your thumb for additional pressure, which can be released instantly in such circumstances.

I fish for fun, and do everything I can to increase my enjoyment when playing a fish. To me, a single action reel provides that extra thrill and I highly recommend everyone at least to give it a try.

90 PRACTISE FIRST

As a charter guide I would often work extremely hard to find the fish and get a good salmon hooked and on the line. Just as I was feeling satisfied with myself, the angler would jam his hand into the reel handles to stop a hard-running fish and it would be gone (usually with one of my favorite lures)!

An exhilarating moment of success was thus turned into an embarrassing failure for the angler who often turned his wrath on me, blaming a weak line, poor knot or improperly oiled reel. I listened to these complaints with a weak smile, knowing that all of these factors had been checked thoroughly beforehand.

Then I began a practice which drastically cut the incidence of lost fish. I asked each neophyte angler to practise playing the fish right on the dock before we headed for the fishing grounds. I would ask him to hold the rod up while I pulled the line and raced up and down the dock like a maniac. They learned proper fish-playing techniques. Surprisingly, it took only a minute or two for most people to get the hang of it.

More recently I have developed a Salmon Simulator to do the same thing in a more sophisticated manner, and use it for training at my fishing classes. It is like a giant video game with the angler standing in front of a large mural depicting a lake or ocean bay setting. Running across the mural is a slot through which the fishing line passes to a mechanical device behind. This device pulls and jerks the line in an extremely realistic manner. It is hooked to a computer which measures line tension and tells the angler how well he is doing.

91 LET HIM RUN

When I was a fishing guide I got just as excited as my customers when a fish struck and was on the line. I would excitedly and continuously shout two pieces of advice. One was "keep your rod up" and the other was "let him run". This is the moment we have been waiting for. We want to enjoy every moment and let the fish run and play, allowing us to feel the surging rod and screaming reel.

Many anglers take fishing so seriously that they can't enjoy their fish. They grind furiously, forcing the fish toward the boat as fast as possible. They somehow feel that getting maximum poundage in the boat as quickly as possible is the purpose of fishing. Realists in the sportsfishing fraternity realize that the actual cost of sport-caught salmon is probably *more than $50 a pound* so, if meat is the object, buy it at the fish market and take up sailing or golf.

Letting the fish run is also sensible from a practical point of view. A fish is easier to handle on a longer line and the stretch of the nylon gives an additional shock absorbing factor. Forcing a fish in quickly leaves you with a wild bucking bronco on a very short line right next to the boat. There is little margin for error in line stretch or even rod action. The fish can also dash frantically under the boat or into the propellers. It is far better to have the salmon tired and docile from lots of running away from the boat.

If you are fishing in a crowd of boats, a long line can be troublesome because other craft can troll right over it and cut off the fish. In this situation it is wise to keep the motor in gear and follow the fish out and away from the crowd.

92 | KEEP THE FISH MOVING

Sometimes a salmon will make a good run then simply "dog it" and just lie out there shaking its head or pulling slowly and firmly against the line.

Big fish will often "sound" to the bottom and just tug away doggedly. We have underwater pictures of fish swimming directly opposite to the direction of the line, just maintaining enough pressure to hold their position but not moving anywhere. In this situation I like to keep the fish moving. Gills are a most inefficient breathing apparatus and they slam shut when the fish swims rapidly. If you can keep the fish moving, it will expend its energy in a more spectacular and enjoyable fight and come to the boat well played out.

Often large chinook will head straight for the bottom and you end up directly above, pulling straight up while the fish tries to bury its nose in the bottom. You can get the fish moving again with several tactics:
• Thump on the butt of the rod with the flat of your palm, transmitting a shock wave through the rod and line to the fish.

• Strum the line by grabbing it just above the reel, pulling it sideways a foot or two, then letting go suddenly with a snap which is transmitted to the fish.

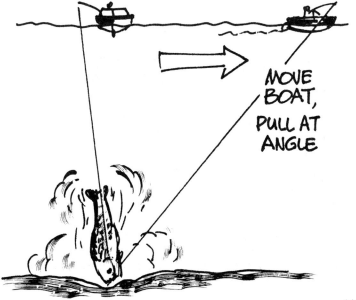

• Probably the most effective tactic is to move the boat off to the side. This allows you to pull at a side angle on the fish, diverting it from its bottom-rubbing maneuver by forcing its head to one side. Usually the fish will take off in a driving run, sometimes heading straight for the surface.

93 PLAY THE FISH TO THE STERN

Using small boats (under about 14 feet in length), it doesn't matter which direction the fish is running. You can swing the rod in any direction to clear the bow or stern as needed. However, larger boats with cabins or canvas and plastic rain covers can be a major problem if the fish runs toward the bow. You may have to put the boat in gear and turn it so that the angler is always facing the fish off the stern of the boat.

If the fish runs under the boat or starts heading across the bow, plunge the rod tip down deep in the water so that the line will clear the hull and propellers. You can then work the line around the stern (with the rod tip straight down) and move to the opposite side of the boat to play the fish in the clear again.

There is one important exception to the rule of "keep the rod up". When a fish jumps close to the boat, the entire line can pop free of the water's surface and run straight from the rod tip to the fish with no line friction from the water. The rod tip will usually spring back straight and the natural tendency for the angler is to pull back farther to maintain a bend in the rod. This leaves a short, taut line which can break or tear out the hooks as the fish drops back into the water. The obvious answer is to drop the rod tip quickly when the fish jumps and allow a momentary slack line, recovering tension immediately as the fish enters the water.

94 STEADY ON THE NET

Many salmon, especially large ones, are lost at the boat when excited anglers try to net them too soon. Thrusting a net at a lively fish usually results in disaster. The fish immediately panics at the sight and sound of the net hitting the water and moving toward it. With one sweep of its powerful tail, the fish can rush off with surprising force and speed, sometimes rushing right past a portion of the net where trailing hooks might catch in the mesh ... and the fish is gone.

The angler on the rod instinctively tries to hold back the rushing fish for the netter, often resulting in broken line or torn out hooks. When bringing a fish to net, I don't usually have my hands on the reel at all, using them instead to guide the rod and the fish toward the net. If the fish runs, the reel is free to spin out.

95 NET THE FISH HEADFIRST

Smaller salmon, under about three pounds, can often be netted by just scooping the net under the fish's body. Larger fish, however, should *always* be netted headfirst. Moreover, the fish should be tired enough so it's lying on its side or back and is relatively easy to control.

96 DO NOT LIFT THE FISH'S HEAD

Do not lift the head out of the water, as this puts additional strain on the rod and can also cause the fish to thrash suddenly when it discovers its gills are clear of the water and it can no longer breathe. Just put enough tension on the rod to keep the salmon's head at the surface, then lead it gently toward the net.

The net should be slid quietly but quickly into the water at about a 45 degree angle. When half the fish's body is over the rim of the net you can slack off the rod tension and the fish will swim right into the bag of the net.

If you attempt to net a fish tail first (even a completely exhausted specimen) it will most likely make one last sweep of the tail when it hits the net mesh. The fish's tail thrusting against the mesh acts just like a diving board and will catapult the fish right out of the net. If some extra hooks happen to be near the mesh they can hang up and tear loose from the fish.

97 DON'T PUT A STRAIN ON THE NET HANDLE

After the fish is in the net, do not lift it like a shovel full of dirt. This puts a tremendous strain on the handle and could likely bend or even break it off.

It is much better to lift the net vertically so the fish is trapped in the bag. Then reach down and grab the rim of the net to lift the fish aboard.

If you want to be *classy*, hit the fish over the head before lifting it into the boat. This prevents it from thrashing around in the net and knocking off scales, and will provide you with a beautiful looking fish to show off.

98 KILL IT CLEANLY

Salmon should be dispatched with a sharp blow right between the eyes. Many fishermen hit the fish too far back on the head which will not necessarily kill it and may leave the angler bashing repeatedly at the twisting, flopping fish. A misplaced blow will also cause a blood bruise in the prime flesh just back of the head.

99 RELEASE SMALL FISH GENTLY

If you hook an undersized fish it will have a far better chance of survival if it is not touched by your hands or even the landing net.

The proper procedure is to grasp the line near the hook and lift the fish out of the water. Then use a small gaff hook or special hook releaser (see illustration) which is slid down the line to the hook and twisted upward so the fish falls free. Many anglers believe that if the fish swims away after release, it has survived. My experience while operating the Undersea Gardens proved otherwise. We often went on fishing expeditions to capture live salmon as specimens for our exhibits. We hooked and landed them with extreme care, placing them live in a large tank with circulating, oxygenated water.

We would put them into the display area in apparently excellent health. But, within three or four days some of them would begin to develop fungus growth, sometimes in the shape of individual fingerprints where they had been held too tightly. Others would show fungus marks corresponding to net abrasion. Within a week or 10 days the fungus would spread into the gill cavity and the fish would die.

I often feel that fishing regulations are unrealistic in forcing anglers to release injured salmon which have no possibility of

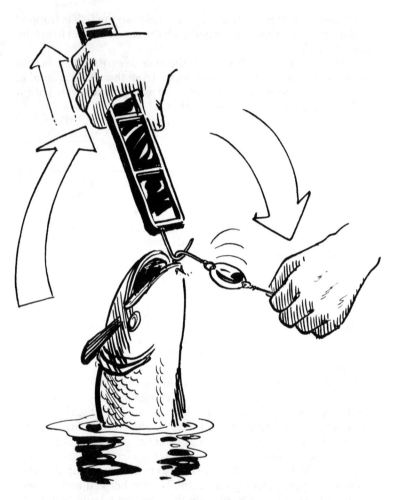

survival, since even those that are handled carefully are quite vulnerable to disease if the protective slime on their skin is disturbed. However, fisheries officers claim, and quite justifiably, that if wounded fish were excepted from the rules, any angler could deliberately injure undersized fish and be within the law in keeping it.

Perhaps the rules should be changed to give fishermen some option in keeping wounded fish and counting them toward his daily limit. It's not a perfect answer, but it seems better than feeding the dogfish and seals.

CARING FOR YOUR FISH

100 Bringing meat home for the frying pan is not the prime purpose of most recreational anglers, but enjoying the harvest of a good day's fishing is certainly one of the great joys of the sport. Fresh salmon is an exquisite delicacy, prized by gourmet chefs all over the world. They would be absolutely shocked to see the way many anglers treat their catch. Listed below are some important *do's* and *don'ts* in taking care of the catch:

• Don't drop the fish on the deck or throw it into a fish box. This will bruise the flesh and soften the meat. This rough handling is one of the reasons why seine-caught commercial fish are worth less than tenderly handled commercial troll fish.

• Bleed your fish. Immediately after dispatching the fish it is a good idea to tear a gill raker loose or slit the fish's throat. This lets it bleed and improves the quality and flavor of the meat. It can be a messy practice, but many anglers believe that it is well worth the trouble.

• Wipe the slime from the fish. In the rough and tumble action of a day's fishing not many anglers bother to wipe down their fish on the fishing grounds, but it should certainly be done during a lull in action or upon returning to the dock.

• Do not store freshly caught fish in plastic bags. There are chemical changes in a fish's body immediately after it's caught and these changes need air circulation, especially before the fish has been cleaned. Fish stored in plastic bags will go soft very quickly.

• Never leave fish in the sun. Fish should be stored in an insulated fish box if possible, with ice or artificial ice packs on top. A wet cloth or burlap bag will serve a similar purpose as evaporation cools the fish. The cloth should be moistened regularly. By all means, keep the fish box in a shaded area if at all possible. If fishing in an open boat you can often cover the fish box with your coat if the weather warms up. You don't need the coat yourself and it will provide the fish with some protection against the sun and heat.

• Keep fish off the bottom of the fish box by using a raised platform. I sometimes use aluminum refrigerator shelving for this purpose. However, any wooden, metal or plastic frame can

be used to hold the fish above the water, blood and slime which gathers in the bottom of a fish box. This fluid will quickly build up in bacteria count, and deteriorate and soften the fish.

If you are using crushed ice (as opposed to artificial plastic pouches) you will need a greater area under the platform to collect the melting ice water.

CLEAN FISH IMMEDIATELY

101 Immediately after returning to shore the fish should be gutted, slime cleaned off and the fish patted dry before storing in plastic bags or newspaper. As soon as you get home the fish should be cut up and put in the refrigerator or stored in plastic bags in the freezer, making sure to squeeze out all air in the bags before freezing.

Some anglers put a water glaze on their fish, especially a trophy salmon they may wish to serve on a special occasion at a later date. Fish can be glazed by sharp-freezing the carcass then spraying it with a fine mist and refreezing. This procedure is repeated several times until a thin glaze of ice builds up around the fish. This keeps it in prime shape for many months.

Chapter 9
Future Plans

I've enjoyed sharing my fishing philosophy, tips and secrets with you. I hope you've gained some information which will help you enjoy your fishing time and catch more fish.

We are still working with our underwater camera to learn even more about fish behavior. In our latest film, "In Search of the Ultimate Lure", we hope to reveal some new information on the basic "triggers" which motivate fish to strike. At time of writing we were also working on two other films, one for the Public Broadcasting System in the United States and another for a major film company. These films will cover studies of trout, bass, pike, panfish and the great tropical game fish such as marlin, sailfish and even the fabled great white shark.

I hope you will be able to see one of my films or read about our new research in an upcoming book.

Tight lines and good fishing!

Your Secrets

_____

_____

_____

_____

_____

_____

_____

_____

_____

_____

_____

_____

Your Secrets

_____

_____

_____

_____

_____

_____

_____

_____

_____

_____

_____

_____

_____

Your Secrets

_____

_____

_____

_____

_____

_____

_____

_____

_____

_____

_____

_____

Your Secrets

_____

_____

_____

_____

_____

_____

_____

_____

_____

_____

_____

_____

_____

Your Secrets

_____

_____

_____

_____

_____

_____

_____

_____

_____

_____

_____

_____

Your Secrets

_____

_____

_____

_____

_____

_____

_____

_____

_____

_____

_____

_____

Date: _____

DATE	TIME	PLACE	TIDE	TIME OF SLACK	WEATHER	LURE

Charlie White's "Fishing Log"

LURE COLOR	LURE DEPTH	DEPTH	FISH CAUGHT	REMARKS

A CUTTHROAT COLLECTION

A guide to Understanding and Catching the Mysterious Trout

The Cutthroat is being restored to fishable quantities by the Salmonid Enhancement Program. Until now little has been written about this popular, but mysterious quarry. This collection fills the void. Noted experts, Bob Jones, Dave Stewart, David Elliott, Ron Nelson, John Massey, Ian Forbes and Karl Bruhn pool their knowledge and experience to unravel the mysteries surrounding this elusive fish and help you understand, conserve, catch and cook it.

Great reading for both fresh and saltwater fishermen.

$5.95

MAKE YOUR OWN FISHING TACKLE
by Bob Jones

Put your hands to work — save money and have fun! Learn how to make your own tackle with well-known expert Bob Jones. Sixteen information-packed chapters cover lures, spoons, spinners, wooden plugs, spinner baits, leadhead jigs, all kinds of molds — and more. There are more than 150 photographs and illustrations to guide you. Plus tips on use and safety. Now you can equip your tackle box for pennies rather than dollars — so you'll be prepared to risk your tackle in snag-filled waters where you previously avoided — and where the fish are usually found!

Make Your Own Fishing Tackle — a small investment to make you a more successful angler!

$8.95 #0128

CHARLIE WHITE'S FISHING SECRETS

Charlie shares more than a hundred of his special fishing secrets to help improve technique and increase your catch. No fisherman can pass this one up! Illustrated throughout with Nelson Dewey's distinctive cartoons and helpful diagrams.

$6.95 #0401

LIVING OFF THE SEA

by Charlie White

A comprehensive look at the bonanza of marine life in the North Pacific. Here are detailed techniques for locating and catching crabs, prawn, shrimp, sole, cod and other bottomfish, oysters, clams and more! And how to clean, fillet, shuck — in fact everything you need to know to enjoy the freshest and tastiest seafood in the world. Illustrated with black-and-white photographs and lots of helpful diagrams.

$6.95 #0142

HOW TO COOK YOUR CATCH
by JEAN CHALLENGER

A great companion for our "How-to-Catch" books! Tells how to cook on board a boat, at a cabin or campsite! Shortcuts in preparing seafood for cooking! Cleaning and filleting! Recipes and methods for preparing delicious meals using simple camp utensils! Special section on exotic seafoods! Illustrated

$2.95

HOW TO CATCH SHELLFISH!
by CHARLES WHITE

How, when and where to find and catch many forms of tasty shellfish! Oysters, Clams, Shrimp, mussels, limpets. Easiest way to shuck oysters. Best equipment for clamming and shrimping! When **not** to eat certain shellfish! **What to eat** and **what to discard!** Easy ways to open and clean shellfish! How to outrace a razor clam. A delightful book chock-full of useful information! Illustrated. **Newly Expanded Edition!**

$2.95

HOW TO CATCH CRABS!
by CAP'N CRABWELLE

Now in a seventh printing, with revisions that show latest crabbing techniques! Tells how to catch crabs with traps, scoops, rings! **Where, when** and **how** to set traps! Best baits! Detailed description and illustrations of a much **easier** method of cleaning, cooking and shelling the meat! A great book, crammed-full of all you need to know about **How to Catch Crabs. Newly Expanded Edition!**

$3.50

WHERE TO FIND SALMON —
Vancouver Island
by ALEC MERRIMAN

Where to Find Salmon combines catch dates and locations of more than 75,000 salmon caught in the season-long "King Fisherman" contest, as well as on-the-spot research, first-hand reports, and "local knowledge". Plus — Detailed maps of the "hot spots", and easy-to-read charts! Know when (and where) the runs arrive in each area, and plan your fishing trips accordingly! Fishermen using the information in this book are finding that the big runs of Salmon are showing up right "on schedule" each year! **New Expanded Edition $4.95**

More great reading designed to ensure your fishing success

All these books are available at your bookstore or sporting goods store — or you can order them directly from BC OUTDOORS on the convenient order form at the end of this book!

HOW TO CATCH SALMON — AD VANCED TECHNIQUES
by CHARLES WHITE & GUEST AUTHORS

The most comprehensive salmon fishing book available! Over 250 pages, crammed full of how-to tips and easy-to-follow diagrams! Covers all popular salmon fishing methods: Downrigger Techniques; Mooching; Trolling with bait; Tricks with Spoons and Plugs; Tips for river mouth fishing; Catching giant Tyees; Winter Fishing; Secrets of Dodger and Flasher fishing; Buzz bombs, Deadly Dicks, Sneaks and other casting lures – AND MUCH MORE!

$5.95

HOW TO CATCH SALMON — BASIC FUNDAMENTALS
by CHARLES WHITE

The most popular salmon book ever written! Contains basic information on trolling patterns, rigging tackle, fisheries Dept. information on most productive lures, proper depths to fish, salmon habit patterns, how to play and net your fish, downriggers, where to find fish! This is the basic book on salmon fishing in the North Pacific and now has been expanded and updated to include the Great Lakes region as well.

$4.95

HOW TO CATCH STEELHEAD!
by ALEC MERRIMAN
Now in a third printing, this book by popular outdoors writer Alec Merriman contains much valuable information for either novice or expert steelheader! Tells how to "read" the water to find steelhead! Proper weight and bait hookups. Bottom-bouncing. How to preserve bait! Techniques for fishing either clear or murky water! Fly fish for Steelhead! Many diagrams and illustrations.

Revised
$2.95

HOW TO CATCH TROUT!
by LEE STRAIGHT
Lee Straight has been fish and game columnist in the Vancouver Sun for more than 28 years. He is regarded as one of Western Canada's top outdoorsmen.
"How to Catch Trout" contains many fish catching "secrets" from his own wide experience and from the experts with whom he has fished! The book contains chapters on Trolling, Still Fishing, Best Equipment, Casting, Ice Fishing, Best Baits and Lures, River and Lake fishing methods — and much more!

$3.95

BUCKTAILS AND HOOCHIES!
by BRUCE COLEGRAVE & JACK GAUNT
Trolling Bucktail flies is one of the most exciting methods of Catching Salmon — as well as being very productive — using the methods described by Bucktail expert Bruce Colegrave.
Hoochies have always been the favorite of commercial fishermen and are catching on rapidly with sportsmen. Commercial expert Jack Gaunt provides a special section on how to catch Salmon with Hoochies.

$2.95

BOOK ORDER FORM
BOOK ORDER FORM

BOOK ORDER FORM

To: **BC Outdoors**
**202-1132 Hamilton Street,
Vancouver, B.C. V6B 2S2**

Please send me the following books:

HOW TO CATCH SALMON – Advanced Techniques	_____ at $5.95	$_____
HOW TO CATCH SALMON – Basic Fundamentals	_____ at $4.95	$_____
HOW TO CATCH STEELHEAD	_____ at $2.95	$_____
HOW TO CATCH TROUT	_____ at $3.95	$_____
HOW TO FISH WITH BUCKTAILS & HOOCHIES	_____ at $2.95	$_____
HOW TO CATCH SHELLFISH	_____ at $2.95	$_____
HOW TO CATCH CRABS	_____ at $3.50	$_____
WHERE TO FIND SALMON	_____ at $4.95	$_____
DRIFTFISHING TECHNIQUES	_____ at $5.95	$_____
HOW TO CATCH BOTTOMFISH	_____ at $2.95	$_____
HOW TO FISH WITH DODGERS & FLASHERS	_____ at $2.95	$_____
A CUTTHROAT COLLECTION	_____ at $5.95	$_____
MAKE YOUR OWN FISHING TACKLE – Volume 1	_____ at $8.95	$_____
CHARLIE WHITE'S FISHING SECRETS	_____ at $6.95	$_____
LIVING OFF THE SEA	_____ at $6.95	$_____
HOW TO COOK YOUR CATCH	_____ at $2.95	$_____
DISCOVER BARKERVILLE	_____ at $6.95	$_____
BOWRON LAKES	_____ at $7.95	$_____
	TOTAL PAGE 1	$_____

TOTAL PAGE 1		$_____
LOGGING ROAD TRAVEL — Volume 1	_____ at $5.95	$_____
PRINCE GEORGE BACKROADS	_____ at $4.95	$_____
OUTDOORS WITH ALEC MERRIMAN	_____ at $3.95	$_____
EXPLORING BRITISH COLUMBIA WATERWAYS	_____ at $4.95	$_____
OKANAGAN BACKROADS — Volume 1	_____ at $3.95	$_____
LOWER MAINLAND BACKROADS — Volume 2 - Fraser Valley	_____ at $4.95	$_____
— Volume 3 - Hope to Clinton	_____ at $4.95	$_____
— Volume 4 - Garibaldi Region	_____ at $4.95	$_____
BACKROADS EXPLORER	_____ at $9.95	$_____
GREAT HUNTING ADVENTURES	_____ at $7.95	$_____
HOW TO HUNT DEER AND OTHER GAME	_____ at $1.95	$_____
Sub Total		$_____
Postage and handling (up to 4 books 50¢ per book, 5 or more 35¢ a book)		$_____
TOTAL		$_____

☐ My cheque for $_____ is enclosed
☐ Visa   ☐ MasterCard

_____
CREDIT CARD NUMBER   EXPIRY DATE

_____
SIGNATURE

_____
NAME (PLEASE PRINT)

_____
ADDRESS

_____
CITY   PROVINCE   POSTAL CODE

ALL PRICES QUOTED ARE CURRENT AT TIME OF GOING TO PRESS.
HOWEVER, AS BOOKS ARE REPRINTED, PRICES MAY CHANGE.